PHILOSOPHERS TAKE ON THE WORLD

Edited by
DAVID EDMONDS

# PHILOSOPHERS TAKE ON THE WORLD

OXFORD
UNIVERSITY PRESS

# OXFORD
### UNIVERSITY PRESS

Great Clarendon Street, Oxford, OX2 6DP,
United Kingdom

Oxford University Press is a department of the University of Oxford.
It furthers the University's objective of excellence in research, scholarship,
and education by publishing worldwide. Oxford is a registered trade mark of
Oxford University Press in the UK and in certain other countries

Published in the United States of America by Oxford University Press
198 Madison Avenue, New York, NY 10016, United States of America

British Library Cataloguing in Publication Data
Data available

Library of Congress Control Number: 2016936520

ISBN 978–0–19–875372–8

Printed in Great Britain by
Clays Ltd, St Ives plc

Links to third party websites are provided by Oxford in good faith and
for information only. Oxford disclaims any responsibility for the materials
contained in any third party website referenced in this work.

# EDITOR'S PREFACE

The point of philosophy, thought Karl Marx, is not just to interpret the world, but to change it. It's an obligation that seems especially relevant to a subcategory within philosophy, Applied Ethics. There doesn't seem much point philosophizing about contested moral issues—whether it be free speech, gun control, euthanasia, or drugs in sport—if it has no influence on debate. Yet, although there's fascinating academic work in all areas of applied moral philosophy, little of it reaches a wider public. The media is full of commentators holding forth on subjects in which philosophers specialize, but philosophers themselves are rarely called upon to comment.

To a large extent that's the fault of philosophers—who often express themselves in abstruse and technical language, inaccessible to anybody beyond the academy. This is not, I hope, a charge that can be levelled at contributors to this book.

All these contributors have an Oxford connection. In Applied Ethics, Oxford University has an outstanding reputation. Much of the credit for this rests with the Uehiro Centre for Practical Ethics. In 2007 the Uehiro Centre set up a daily blog in which philosophers give their take on a story in the news. The *Practical Ethics Blog* has now had nearly two thousand posts, which have had millions of page views. For the Uehiro Centre the blog has become a central part of its outreach activities, showcasing its work to a broader public. It's also proved a fertile and experimental outlet for ideas. A blog is the antithesis of a peer-reviewed journal. The *Practical Ethics Blog* has given philosophers the opportunity to float new, often counter-intuitive arguments, and in a more free-flowing style than would be appropriate in an academic publication. Many posts appearing in this book have gone on to have an afterlife after being picked up elsewhere in the media.

This book is a selection from the best and most thought-provoking posts. Some of these posts appear here little altered from their original; many others have been substantially reworked.

This volume covers many topics in moral philosophy but, of course, it's necessarily selective. Research at the Uehiro Centre focuses not just on perennial topics in morality, but emerging ones too. And so it's not surprising that one significant strand in this book is how we should deal with novel dilemmas thrown up by our modern world: internet shaming, three biological-parent families, enhancement drugs. Often these problems are particularly taxing, since advances in science and technology seem to outpace the intuitions we have to deal with them. But that also gives them particular urgency.

Almost all of the posts were inspired by some event in the news. In writing about moral philosophy, philosophers typically use not real cases but thought-experiments, often highly stylized thought-experiments: the runaway train that is going to kill five people unless you flick a switch to turn it down a spur, where one person is tied to the track and will die. A common charge levelled at these thought-experiments is that they are absurdly unrealistic. Our intuitions about thought-experiments, critics say, cannot be transplanted in any useful way back onto the real world.

The cases discussed in this book don't just bear a resemblance to real life, they *are* real life. That presents a moral conundrum of its own. Behind these philosophical musings are true stories about real people, people who deserve better than to have their stories coldly and intellectually dissected as if by a pathologist performing an autopsy. All the writers here have, I believe, treated the subjects of their discussion with appropriate respect. But ultimately, practical ethics, if it's to serve any useful function, has to be about real people with real feelings who face real troubles and real dilemmas.

The *Practical Ethics Blog*, meanwhile, is ongoing. You can access it at <http://blog.practicalethics.ox.ac.uk>

DAVID EDMONDS, AUGUST 2016
*@davidedmonds100*

# ACKNOWLEDGEMENTS

When the idea of this book came up—a book requiring cooperation from numerous philosophers—the term 'herding cats' sprang immediately to mind.

My fears were unwarranted. Contributors in this volume range from philosophers with international reputations to those just starting out on their academic careers. They have, without exception, been a delight to work with. My thanks to them all.

Although it was my job to make the initial selection of posts, several philosophers acted as referees to provide a valuable second opinion. So I owe a debt of gratitude to Steve Clarke, Roger Crisp, Tom Douglas, Brian Earp, Neil Levy, Hannah Maslen, Ingmar Persson, Janet Radcliffe Richards, Rebecca Roache, Julian Savulescu, and Dominic Wilkinson.

For 8 years now I have been privileged to hold a senior research fellowship at Oxford's Uehiro Centre for Practical Ethics. I would like to thank all the administrative staff at the centre, particularly Rachel Gaminiratne, Deborah Sheehan, Rocci Wilkinson, and Miriam Wood. The *sine qua non* of the centre is Director Julian Savulescu, who first proposed this book and who has enthusiastically championed it throughout. Most of all, I would like to thank the Uehiro Foundation on Ethics and Education for making all this possible by the generous support to the centre and all its staff.

I would like to thank Veronique Baxter at David Higham; my mother, Hannah Edmonds, for copyediting, as usual; and the OUP team, Matthias Butler, Eleanor Collins, Lisa Eaton, Jen Moore, and rock-star editor Peter Momtchiloff.

'Why, why, why?' Good questions. This book is dedicated to budding philosophers Saul and Isaac Edmonds.

# CONTENTS

## Health and medicine

## Drugs and organs

## Religion and charity

# Sport

# Brains

# Language, speech, and freedom

## Evil, disgust, shame, rudeness, and joy

## Animals

## The future and its people

# CRIME AND PUNISHMENT

# 1

# TIME TO RECONSIDER
# THE PENAL CODE?

Anders Herlitz

R ecently a number of websites have sprung up devoted to publicly
exposing convicted criminals.

Some sites claim that their purpose is to 'shame' criminals, others that
it's to make available information that will improve public safety. Some
sites are legal and operate within the law, others violate the law.

Exposure of ex-convicts has now been taken to a new level in Sweden
with the launch of the website Lexbase.[1] The site gave users the opportunity to search a big database of court decisions for individuals, companies,
or ID numbers, and then to look at maps with red dots indicating where
ex-convicts reside. The database consisted of all convictions in Sweden
over the last 5 years. For a small fee (around £5/$8), users could purchase
detailed information about an individual case. The site was an immediate hit. Within two days, it had had 3 million visitors (the Swedish
population is just below 10 million). On the third day, the site was
hacked[2] and the information was made freely available on other websites. On the fourth day, the internet service provider closed the site after
criticism in the media, from the government and from the public, about
security threats, while its complete database was made available on the
file-sharing site The Pirate Bay.

As I say, Lexbase is extreme, but not alone. In the UK there is a website
listing child abusers; it too allows users to see where former criminals (in
this case, sex offenders) reside. Likewise, CriminalCheck.com, in the US,
allows you to search for national sex offenders. Other websites focus on
certain groups in society. There are racist organizations that provide
information on criminals with certain ethnic backgrounds.

It seems unlikely that legislators, even if they wished to do so, could prevent this information from being disseminated. But the consequences for ex-convicts span from mildly upsetting to absolutely devastating. It is perhaps only slightly embarrassing if your neighbours discover that in your youth you were convicted for shoplifting. But if you have been found guilty of child molesting? Who wants a child molester as a tenant? Who wants to hire him? Who wants to be his friend? The consequences of these sites constitute an extra-juridical punishment for convicts who have already done their time.

This is new. The internet has facilitated the generalization of a phenomenon that used to require the traditional media and was confined to rare cases usually involving celebrities. The old media would splash juicy crime stories on its pages—Roman Polanski's statutory rape conviction or George Michael soliciting a policeman—but 99% of cases went unreported. In effect, what we see now is the potential normalization of two parallel, historically mutually exclusive, punitive standards. The first, the current penal code, has its roots in modernity and the shift from corporal punishment to institutional incarceration. The second relies on mob mentality and human instincts of disgust and revenge to ostracize and humiliate criminals.

All this raises an important question. Should the juridical system take the consequences of extra-judicial penalties into account in determining punishment?

If we invoke the widespread idea that a crime ought to be punished with a fixed punishment, the duality of punitive systems is deeply problematic. If a court sentenced a rapist to jail a few years ago, the principal punishment was the length of the sentence. Today, a court that sentences a rapist to prison in effect condemns him to incarceration plus the effects for the criminal of inclusion in any potential sex-offender database; for example, difficulty in finding a job and a place to live, public humiliation, and social ostracism. In other words, a sentence previously equivalent to punishment X, today is X+Y. Consistency suggests we ought to discount for Y.

Discounting for the extra-juridical punishment (Y) can be done in at least two ways. Either we adjust our penal code or court practices to take into account the expected extra-juridical punishments, or we compensate convicts for the unintended yet predictable outcomes of convictions. Thus, the consequences for a rapist of being included on exposure websites could be established to be commensurate to 6 months in prison, and the punishment lowered accordingly. Or we could provide some benefit to the convict in compensation for Y. For example, the same rapist could be given tax relief for a set number of years, or extended unemployment benefits, or priority in the allocation of social housing.

It is true that the consequences from public exposure from the court convicting a criminal might be unintended by the court. But at least two generally accepted ethical principles give us reason to discount for unintended, predictable outcomes: proportionality and consistency. Popular and theoretical conceptions of justice hold that punishments sanctioned by the state should stand in relation—in proportion—to the crime committed. The introduction of extra-juridical punishments represents an increase in punishment, and proportionality requires that this be taken into account. Another widely accepted idea with solid theoretical grounding is that identical crimes should be met with identical punishments, over time and space. If information technology means that an identical sentence is a worse punishment now than 20 years ago, consistency entails that we factor this in.

An alternative stance would be to accept the extra-juridical punishment, and insist that this is what sex offenders, murderers, and thieves deserve. Yet, if this path is taken, we should at the very least be honest about it. We should recognize that we are condemning criminals to a significant increase of punishment, and that our society has taken a turn toward embracing and applying both medieval and modern standards of punitive justice simultaneously.

## Notes

1. <http://digitaljournal.com/news/world/swedish-website-publishes-criminal-records/article/367829>
2. <http://sverigesradio.se/sida/artikel.aspx?programid=2054&artikel=5770189>

## 2

# ENHANCED PUNISHMENT

*Can technology make life sentences longer?*

Rebecca Roache

In August 2013 the mother and stepfather of Daniel Pelka each received a life sentence for his murder.[1] Daniel was four when he died in March 2012. In his last few months he was beaten, starved, held under water until he lost consciousness, denied medical treatment, locked in a tiny room containing only a mattress on which he was expected both to sleep and defecate, humiliated, denied affection, and subjected to grotesquely creative abuse such as being force-fed salt when he asked for a drink of water. His young sibling witnessed much of this, and neighbours reported hearing Daniel's screams at night.

Daniel's mother, Magdelena Luczak, and stepfather, Mariusz Krezolek, have both died in prison since their sentencing. Advocates of the death penalty will argue that this is no more than they deserve. But what if Luczak and Krezolek hadn't died? Do justice systems that do not incorporate the death penalty have the resources to punish such crimes appropriately?

Had they lived, Luczak and Krezolek would each have served a minimum of 30 years in prison. The conditions in which they would have served their sentences must, by law, meet certain standards. Prisoners must be fed and watered, given clean cells, access to a toilet and washing facilities, access to medical treatment, and allowed out of their cells for exercise and recreation. Luczak and Krezolek denied Daniel all of these things. If you are a retributivist, this is concerning. The UK's punishment system is primarily retributive. In a retributive system, just punishments are proportionate punishments. Yet Luczak and Krezolek's punishments were not proportionate to their crimes. Can anything be done about this?

Some argue that retributive punishment should be replaced with a forward-looking approach such as restorative justice.[2] I won't discuss that here. I want to consider how *retributivists* might address the problem that, in some cases, it is not possible to make punishment proportionate if it is to be both humane and restricted by current human life expectancy.

Retributivists could turn to technology for ways to increase the severity of punishments without making drastic changes to the current UK legal system. Here are some possibilities.

*Lifespan enhancement:* Many transhumanists believe that science will soon enable humans to remain healthy indefinitely. Aubrey de Grey, co-founder of the anti-ageing Sens research foundation, believes that the first person to live 1,000 years is already alive.[3] In cases where a 30-year life sentence is judged too lenient, convicted criminals could be sentenced to receive a life sentence in conjunction with lifespan enhancement. As a result, life imprisonment could mean several hundred years rather than a few decades. It would, of course, be more expensive for society to support such sentences. However, if lifespan enhancement were widely available, this cost could be offset by the increased contributions of a longer-living workforce.

*Mind uploading:* As the technology required to scan and map human brain processes improves,[4] some believe it will become possible to upload minds to computers.[5] We could then speed up the uploaded mind. Nick Bostrom calls a vastly faster version of human-level intelligence 'speed superintelligence'. He observes that a speed superintelligence, operating at 10,000 times that of a biological brain, 'would be able to read a book in a few seconds and write a PhD thesis in an afternoon. If the speed-up were instead a factor of a million, a millennium of thinking would be accomplished in eight and a half hours'.[6] Uploading the mind of a convicted criminal and running it a million times faster than normal would enable the uploaded criminal to serve a 1,000 year sentence in eight and a half hours.

*Altering perception of duration:* Various factors can cause people to perceive time as passing more slowly. These include our emotional state,[7] the emotional state we witness in others,[8] psychoactive drugs,[9] mindfulness meditation,[10] and body temperature.[11] Time seems to pass more slowly for children than for adults, which may relate to attention and information processing.[12] Such insights could inform the design and management of prisons, so that even without increasing the real-time length of sentences, they could be made subjectively longer.

*Robot prison officers*: Consideration of the welfare of prison staff limits how unpleasant prison can be made for prisoners. If human staff could one day be replaced by robots, this limiting factor would be removed. Robotics technology has already produced *self-driving cars*,[13] which places robot prison officers within the bounds of possibility. Being overseen by robots rather than other human beings might in and of itself be worse for prisoners.

Of course, all these options raise questions about whether enhanced punishments are humane, and of what constitutes humane punishments more generally. It is important to debate these questions before punishment is technologically enhanced. But, for those who take retributivist punishment seriously, technology offers potentially attractive ways to improve justice.

# Notes

1. <http://www.bbc.co.uk/news/uk-england-23544717>
2. <http://en.wikipedia.org/wiki/Restorative_justice>
3. <http://www.ted.com/talks/aubrey_de_grey_says_we_can_avoid_aging.html>
4. <http://www.fhi.ox.ac.uk/wp-content/uploads/brain-emulation-roadmap-report1.pdf>
5. <https://en.wikipedia.org/wiki/Mind_uploading>
6. Bostrom, N. (2010). 'Intelligence explosion: groundwork for a strategic analysis'. Unpublished manuscript.
7. Droit-Volet, S., Fayolle, S.L., and Gil, S. (2011). 'Emotion and time perception: effects of film-induced mood', *Frontiers in Integrative Neuroscience* 5: 33.
8. Gil, S. and Droit-Volet, S. (2011). 'How do emotional facial expressions influence our perception of time?', in Masmoudi, S., Yan Dai, D., and Naceur, A. (eds) *Attention, Representation, and Human Performance: Integration of Cognition, Emotion and Motivation* (London: Psychology Press, Taylor & Francis).
9. Wittmann, M., Carter, O., Hasler, F., Cahn, B.R., Grimberg, U., Spring, P., Hell, D., Flohr, H., and Vollenweider, F.X. (2007). 'Effects of psilocybin on time perception and temporal control of behaviour in humans', *Journal of Psychopharmacology* 21/1: 50–64.
10. Kramer, R.S., Weger, U.W., and Sharma, D. (2013). 'The effect of mindfulness meditation on time perception', *Consciousness and Cognition* 22/3: 846–52.
11. Wearden, J.H. and Penton-Voak, I.S. (1995). 'Feeling the heat: body temperature and the rate of subjective time, revisited', *The Quarterly Journal*

*of Experimental Psychology Section B: Comparative and Physiological Psychology* 48/2: 129–41.

12. Gruber, R.P., Wagner, L.F. and Block, R.A. (2000). 'Subjective time versus proper (clock) time', in Saniga, M., Buccheri, R., and Di Gesù, V. (eds) *Studies on the Structure of Time: From Physics to Psycho(patho)logy* (New York: Kluwer Academic/Plenum Publishers).

13. <http://www.robots.ox.ac.uk/~mobile/wikisite/pmwiki/pmwiki.php>

# 3

# DEGREES OF SEXUAL HARM

## Brian D. Earp

S hould abortions be allowed in the case of rape?[1] Republican Todd Akin—in the course of his 2012 US Senate campaign—argued that they should not be. His reasoning was as follows:

> From what I understand from doctors, [pregnancy resulting from rape is] really rare. If it's a legitimate rape, the female body has ways to try to shut that whole thing down. But let's assume that maybe that didn't work or something. I think there should be some punishment. But the punishment ought to be of the rapist, and not attacking the child.[2]

In fact, there appears to be no scientific basis for the claim that the trauma of forced intercourse can interrupt ovulation or in any other way prevent a pregnancy. The American Congress of Obstetricians and Gynecologists (ACOG) issued a statement:

> Recent remarks by a member of the US House of Representatives suggesting that 'women who are victims of "legitimate rape" rarely get pregnant' are medically inaccurate, offensive, and dangerous ... Any person forced to submit to sexual intercourse against his or her will is the victim of rape, a heinous crime. There are no varying degrees of rape. To suggest otherwise is inaccurate and insulting and minimizes the serious physical and psychological repercussions for all victims of rape.[3]

There is something curious about this press release. In addition to setting the factual record straight, which the ACOG is well-positioned to do, it adds opinions about how 'offensive' and 'insulting' Akin's remarks were, while declaring that there are no 'degrees of rape'.

I believe that this is a problem. In fact, I think that the ACOG's choice of words may actually serve to undermine the vital efforts of anti-rape advocates to reduce the incidence of sexual assault.

## No degrees of rape?

Let us start with the assertion that there are no 'degrees of rape'. One can guess that this was meant to refute the notion of 'legitimate rape' or real rape, which seems to imply the existence of other kinds—or 'degrees'—of rape that (by contrast) should not be considered 'legitimate' (or real). In using this term, Akin apparently intended to refer to rape that is particularly violent or traumatic, since, on the discredited 'rape shuts down pregnancy' theory, it is meant to be extreme stress that triggers the body's defences.

But whatever the 'no degrees of rape' phrase was *intended* to mean, I think that it may unwittingly cause problems for anti-rape advocacy.

Rape is something that has to be defined. Indeed, it has been defined in a number of different ways across jurisdictions and over time. The FBI used to define rape as 'the carnal knowledge of a female forcibly and against her will'. Now it defines it as 'the penetration, no matter how slight, of the vagina or anus with any body part or object, or oral penetration by a sex organ of another person, without the consent of the victim'.[4] The United Nations has its own definition; so does the World Health Organization; and so on.

Moreover, there are many different *types* of rape (on some classifications), which take into account things like the motivation behind the rape, the relationship between the perpetrator and the victim, the context of the rape, the method of the rape, and so on. There are also clearer and less clear crossings of the boundary of consent, as well as more and less intentional violations of another's sexual autonomy.[5]

Now, it seems beyond dispute that a person's physical and psychological response to rape might vary tremendously depending upon these and other factors. However, this is something that the 'no degrees of rape' claim—in conjunction with the ACOG's description of rape as a 'heinous' crime with 'repercussions for all victims' (as though 'all' victims have a similar experience)—may actually serve to obscure. Indeed, rape is *not* a unitary, metaphysically determined category: it is a value-laden, socio-legally defined phenomenon. Its causes are many and its effects are many. Rape is complicated.

# The question of sexual harm

Why does this matter? One reason it matters is that some people do not realize the *range* of sexual acts, nor the range of situations in which they occur, that have the potential to cause serious harm to another person. To talk about rape as a monolithic thing that doesn't vary—and that unfailingly causes 'serious physical and psychological' harm, as the ACOG press release suggests—does much to play into the cartoon of rape that occurs in dark alleyways, perpetrated by a stranger at gunpoint. Take this satirical skewering of Akin and his comments by *The Onion* as a case in point:

> *Pregnant Woman Relieved To Learn Her Rape Was Illegitimate*
>
> Though she was initially upset following the brutal sexual assault last month that left her pregnant, victim Martha Byars told reporters she was relieved Sunday to learn from Rep. Todd Akin (R-MO) that her ability to conceive her unwanted child proves she was not, in fact, legitimately raped.
>
> 'Being violently coerced into having sex was the worst thing that's ever happened to me, so I take comfort in knowing it wasn't actually rape', Byars said of the vicious encounter in which she was accosted in an alleyway by a stranger, pinned to the ground, and penetrated against her will for 25 minutes. 'It was absolutely horrific—I felt violated in the worst way imaginable—but thanks to Congressman Akin, I now realize it must, at some level, have been consensual after all.'[6]

The intention of this satire is clear, and its grim point is more or less effectively conveyed. But it also highlights a problem with the discourse surrounding rape in our society, which turns on a collective mental picture of rape as being the sort of thing experienced by *The Onion*'s Martha Byars. However, that is not the only sort of sex that counts as rape legally; and it is not the only sort of sex that causes problems morally.

When a person is penetrated sexually without consenting to it, the person doing the penetrating is very rarely a stranger. According to one source,[7] the statistics break down like this:

- Someone with whom the respondent was in love: 46%
- Someone whom the respondent knew well: 22%
- An acquaintance: 19%
- A spouse: 9%
- A stranger: 4%

So we need to move away from the 'stranger in an alleyway' model of rape, and think about the sorts of harm(s) that can occur from unconsented sex between acquaintances, friends, lovers, husbands and wives, etc.

The moral goal is clear. It should be that whenever sex occurs, both parties want it (and are competent to agree to it). On the far end of missing this goal is a violent attack at gunpoint. Somewhere in the middle might be a non-violent, alcohol-fueled encounter between people who desire to have sex and mutually agree to it, but whose capacity to give unambiguously valid consent is diminished on account of their drinking. And on the near end might be a partner who verbally consents to sex even though he's not in the mood. Harmful sex—definitions of rape to one side—can take many forms, and the degree of harm is *not* the same across the board.

Indeed, the psychological impact of various forms of non-consensual sex might range pretty widely. And not necessarily in ways that can first come to mind. If a friend or partner pushes sex, for example, this violation of trust might have a profound effect on the victim—possibly even more profound than if the sexual act were forced on one by a stranger. Furthermore, a great deal of harmful sex occurs when the person doing the penetrating doesn't think of the act as rape—likely because they assume that 'real' rape is the sort of thing that only scary criminals do while brandishing a weapon.

## Conclusion

If we want there to be less sexual harm in the world, then we need to think about the manifold ways that harm can come about, and contribute to a discussion of rape that gets men and women thinking seriously about consent in places other than alleyways. We need some nuance. While the ACOG statement was surely well-intentioned, its 'offended' tone and its portrayal of rape as something that doesn't admit of any degrees, as something that is 'heinous' in all its manifestations, and that inevitably causes serious harm, paradoxically calls to mind a model of rape—the 'stranger' model used by *The Onion*—that actually *obscures* the more complex range of harms that can occur in the messy real world of sexual interaction.

# Notes

1. For a longer version of this piece, see Earp, B. D. (2015), '"Legitimate rape," moral coherence, and degrees of sexual harm'. *Think* 14/41: 9–20.
2. Jaco, C. (19 August 2012). Full interview with Todd Akin. *Jaco Report*. <http://fox2now.com/2012/08/19/the-jaco-report-august-19-2012/>
3. ACOG (20 August 2012). Statement on rape and pregnancy. <http://www.acog.org/About-ACOG/News-Room/News-Releases/2012/Statement-on-Rape-and-Pregnancy>
4. FBI (11 December 2014). 'Frequently asked questions about the change in the UCR definition of rape'. <https://www.fbi.gov/about-us/cjis/ucr/recent-program-updates/new-rape-definition-frequently-asked-questions>
5. Earp, B. D. (28 September 2015). '1 in 4 women: how the latest sexual assault statistics were turned into click bait by the *New York Times*. *Huffington Post*. <http://www.huffingtonpost.com/brian-earp/1-in-4-women-how-the-late_b_8191448.html>
6. Anonymous (20 August 2012). 'Pregnant woman relieved to learn her rape was illegitimate'. *The Onion*. <http://www.theonion.com/articles/pregnant-woman-relieved-to-learn-her-rape-was-ille,29258/?ref=auto>
7. Rathus, S. A., Nevid, J. S., and Fichner-Rathus, L. (1997). *Human Sexuality in a World of Diversity* (Boston, MA: Allyn & Bacon).

# TERRORISM, GUNS, AND WAR

# 4

# A CHALLENGE TO GUN RIGHTS

Jeff McMahan

O n this day in the US, around thirty people will be killed with a gun, not including suicides. Many more will be wounded. I can safely predict this number because that is the average number of homicides committed with a gun in the US each day. Such killings have become so routine that they are barely noticed even in the local news. Only when a significant number of people are murdered, particularly when they include children or are killed randomly, is the event considered newsworthy.

Yet efforts to regulate the possession of guns in the US are consistently defeated.

The case for gun rights rests primarily on two claims: one about facts, the other about moral principle. The factual claim is that members of society as a whole are safer when more of them have guns. This is because, the more reasonable it is for aggressors to believe that potential victims are armed, the more likely it is that these aggressors will be deterred. The claim about principle is that each person has a right of self-defence and that this right entails a further right not to be deprived of, or prevented from having, the most effective means of self-defence. These claims are independent. Most of those who assert them think the second would be true even if the first were false.

Advocates of gun rights (to whom I will refer as 'advocates') usually defend their factual assertion by appealing to statistical claims, such as that, when a city bans handguns, rates of violent crime and homicide increase rather than decrease. The claim about principle is often defended by appeal to an analogy with an individual case. Suppose a person is about to be killed by a culpable aggressor, but has a gun that she can use to defend herself. As the aggressor approaches, another person takes the potential victim's gun away from her, with the consequence that she is killed by the aggressor. It is clear that the intervening person violates the victim's right of defence. The same is true, according to advocates, of a state that deprives its citizens of their guns, or prevents them from having guns. Whenever a person is harmed who could have defended herself if she had had a gun, and her lacking a gun is attributable to restrictions the state imposes on their possession, the state has violated her right of self-defence.

There is much that one could say about each of these claims. The statistics cited above, for example, do not show what happens when an area changes from one in which private citizens have guns to one in which they do not; at most they show what happens when cooperative people surrender their guns, but determined criminals keep theirs. One might add that if advocates in the US really believed their own statistics, they would not have acted so determinedly to stifle government funding for empirical research on gun violence (which they did with great success). As for the example intended to support the claim about principle, there are various failures of analogy between disarming a victim faced with an immediate threat and limiting or prohibiting private possession of guns throughout a society. The relevant analogy is with a situation in which a third party disarms both the aggressor and the potential victim and provides protection for the victim.

I will, however, present a different challenge to the central claims of advocates. I suggest that we test them by imagining a situation in which individuals are continuously at high risk of being wrongly attacked and even killed, but in which the state aggressively prevents them from having guns, or indeed any means of self-defence at all. Instead the state compels them to rely for their security on third-party defenders who, like the police in domestic society, cannot be continuously present to protect them. What advocates say scathingly of the police—'when every second counts, the police are only minutes away'—is often true of these third-party defenders. The central claims of advocates ought to apply most forcefully to people in these conditions. It seems that such people, who are in constant danger of being wrongly attacked or killed, would be safer if they had guns to protect themselves and that the state violates their rights of self-defence by preventing them from having guns and confiscating guns from any who might acquire them.

I think, however, that this is false. Contemporary moral philosophers are noted, or perhaps notorious, for their use of hypothetical examples. The example I have just sketched is hypothetical. But it describes the conditions in an actual institution: prison.

Prison populations contain an unusually high proportion of people who are disposed to violence. And prison inmates often sort themselves into rival groups or gangs that reflect their affiliations prior to imprisonment, thereby importing pre-existing antagonisms into the prison environment. Without protection, prisoners, especially the weaker ones, would be far more likely to be assaulted than most people who are not imprisoned. Yet the state denies them any means of self-defence, forcing them to rely on armed guards and certain physical and institutional safeguards for their protection.

If the logic behind the advocates' claim were correct, prisoners would be safer if they were allowed to have guns and thus did not have to rely on guards for protection. Each would be deterred from attacking any other by the knowledge that the other was, or at least might be, armed. This parallels the advocate's claim that citizens are safer if they are armed and do not have to rely solely on the police for their protection. Of course, if prisoners were armed, they might in many instances be able to defend themselves against guards, thereby decreasing the effectiveness of guards as protectors. But advocates presumably advance their empirical claim in the awareness that police would similarly be more often deterred or forcibly prevented from fulfilling their protective functions if most or all citizens were armed at all times.

It does not take much imagination to see that prisoners locked up together with guns, with or without guards, would not be more secure than prisoners without guns, but with guards. This is particularly obvious in the case of any prisoners who did not have guns when others did. The idea that only some prisoners might have guns is entirely consistent with the gun-rights position. Advocates typically claim only that the right of self-defence entails a right not to be deprived of a gun, or not to be prevented from acquiring one. They do not argue that people have a positive right to be provided with a gun by the state. Their view thus seems to imply that, while the state ought not to prevent prisoners from acquiring guns, it need not provide guns to those who cannot get them otherwise. Those who are unable to get a gun would then have to rely for protection on someone else who has one, just as in the advocates' ideal society those who are unable to acquire or use a gun, such as children and certain disabled people, would have to rely on the generosity of others for their protection.

Advocates will no doubt respond by denying that their view commits them to the claim that the state violates prisoners' rights of self-defence by denying them access to guns. They might, for example, argue that convicted criminals have forfeited their right to the possession of a gun. Yet no one can forfeit his right of self-defence against *wrongful* attack. Consider a modification of the advocates' own example. Suppose a convicted criminal—a former mafia member released temporarily for humanitarian reasons and carrying a gun entirely in anticipation of an attempted 'hit'—will be wrongly killed by a hitman unless he uses his gun in self-defence. Someone who then takes his gun away, thereby ensuring that he is killed, seems to violate his right of self-defence. That might not be true if the criminal would, after defending himself, use the gun to threaten innocent people. Similarly, prisoners might forfeit their right to effective means of self-defence if they could also use those means to threaten innocent people outside of prison. But it does not seem that they forfeit their right to effective means of defending themselves from wrongful attacks by other prisoners.

It seems obvious, however, that the state does not violate the rights of prisoners by denying them access to guns for self-defence. This is particularly clear if each prisoner has a higher expected level of security against assault and homicide when they are all protected by guards than each would have if all were allowed to have guns for self-defence. The right of self-defence is not fundamental, but is derivative from the more basic right to physical security. Thus a prohibition of gun possession does not violate prisoners' rights if it enhances their security by reducing the occasions on which a prisoner might need a gun to defend his life. And the same is true outside of prisons, where, at least in the US, people are more likely to be murdered than they would be if they were in prison.[1]

## Note

1. In the US the murder rate in 2011 was 4.7 per 100,000 people. In local jails between 2000 and 2010 it was 3 per 100,000. See Brian Palmer (19 June 2013). 'Which is safer: city streets or prison?' *Slate.* <http://www.slate.com/articles/news_and_politics/explainer/2013/06/murder_rate_in_prison_is_it_safer_to_be_jailed_than_free.html>

# 5

# McMAHAN'S HAZARDOUS (AND IRRELEVANT) THOUGHT EXPERIMENT

Allen Buchanan and Lance K. Stell

McMahan says that the case for gun ownership rests on two claims: one empirical, the other moral. The empirical claim is that we are safer the more guns there are in private hands. The moral claim is that if someone suffers from an unjust attack under conditions in which the state has denied her access to guns, then the government has violated her right of self-defence. But neither claim is needed to make the case in favour of gun ownership. To make a sound case for gun ownership one needs only: 1) a presumption that people should not be deprived of the means for exercising the right of armed self-defence; 2) a rebuttal of the claim that the presumption is defeated.

McMahan tries to refute the factual claim by recourse to an analogy between prisons and society. He says that allowing inmates to possess guns would make them all less safe and that this shows that by depriving them of access to guns the state does not violate their rights of self-defence. The analogy is flawed.

First of all, one could argue that, by virtue of their crimes, inmates have forfeited some elements of the right of armed self-defence, includ-ing the right to access to firearms.[1] McMahan swiftly dismisses this possibility with the remark that no one can forfeit his right of self-defence against unjust attacks. He gives no reason why this is so, but the question is not whether one can forfeit one's right of self-defence against unjust attacks, but whether one can forfeit one's right to access to guns. Further, if it were true that one cannot forfeit one's access to means for successful defence against unjust attacks, then it would follow that imprisonment massively violates the right of self-defence—after all, if one is in prison then one can't flee one's attacker and one is also deprived of access to guns. But if prison massively violates inmates' right of self-defence that undercuts McMahan's prison analogy strategy.

Second, the situation of inmates is different from that of the general population. They are in a state of abject dependence on the authorities. The law recognizes this by acknowledging a duty of care and protection on the part of the authorities.[2] In contrast, the law explicitly denies that the police have a duty to protect individuals against lethal assault even in a courthouse,[3] presumably in recognition of the fact that the police cannot fully protect us. Where the state has a duty to protect a group because of its special condition of abject state-imposed dependence, it makes good sense to say that they need not have access to the means of self-defence; but that is compatible with saying that when individuals are not in a condition of imposed dependency and where the police have no duty to protect them, they should have access to means of self-defence.

Third, the prison population is relevantly different from the population at large: it contains a higher percentage of persons who have committed murder or assault. McMahan ignores differences between inmates and the general population and, more importantly, between perpetrators of gun violence and the general population, because he thinks that mere access to guns makes ordinary people dangerous—that we would frequently be overcome by passion and engage in gun violence if we had access to guns. McMahan cites no evidence to support this prediction and the evidence speaks against it. According to the Department of Justice, the US homicide rate has declined by 50% since 1980 while gun ownership has skyrocketed. Further, every state now allows concealed carry of firearms, with the number of ordinary people carrying guns increasing dramatically, yet there has been no increase in gun violence. These facts show that most of us are not potential murderers, poised to explode in homicidal rage, thwarted only by our lack of access to guns.

The fourth flaw in the prison analogy is that prisons are tightly controlled environments in which the authorities can prevent at least some of the bad unintended consequences of a ban on gun ownership in society at large. Take another analogy: prohibition. The ban on alcohol in society at large had quite different and much worse consequences than the ban on it in prisons. So we shouldn't assume that banning guns in society at large would be as beneficial as banning them in the tightly controlled prison environment.

McMahan thinks that banning guns in prisons is justifiable because doing so makes inmates safer than they would be if they were allowed to own guns. Since he offers no qualification, he appears to be committed to the thesis that the state can justifiably deprive one of something whenever one would be safer without it. That is repugnant, since it implies that the state may justifiably ban all sorts of items that we all think it shouldn't, including skis, cars, aeroplanes, power tools, swimming pools, squash racquets, alcohol, and libidos. All of these items are dangerous and some (especially cars) produce as many deaths as firearms.

As surprising as his failure to acknowledge any of these relevant differences between prisons and society is McMahan's silence on the problem of unintended bad consequences of a ban on gun ownership. These include a flourishing black market for guns, with predictable burgeoning of organized crime and corruption of law-enforcement personnel (the analogy with the war on drugs is apt here). In addition, it is likely that law-abiding citizens would become less safe than scofflaws,[4] which seems unfair. McMahan ignores the Problem of the Second Best: he wrongly assumes that if a fully effective ban (as can be achieved in a prison) would be a good thing, then the *attempt* to ban guns (in society) would also be a good thing.

That, then, deals with the empirical claim that we are safer the more guns there are in private hands. As we have shown, one simply doesn't need that claim to argue against a ban on private ownership of guns. What of McMahan's criticism of the moral claim? He thinks it's obvious that if we would be safer without gun ownership, the state does not violate our rights of self-defence if it deprives us of access to guns in situations in which we suffer violence that we could have avoided if we had had access. The problem is that he has not shown that we would be safer if there were a ban on gun ownership; at most he has shown that we would be safer if there were a fully effective ban combined with fully effective police protection against assault. So he has not refuted the common-sense idea that if one has a right of self-defence, then no one should deprive one of the effective means for self-defence, if the government cannot fully protect one. Even if we would all be safer if there were no guns in private hands (and assuming effective protection by the police), it is hard to see how that is relevant to whether we should attempt to ban private ownership, since any such attempt will not result in their being no guns in private hands, but will result in some rather severely negative, unintended consequences. And given that, as the statistics show, more guns does not mean more violence, we can't assume that *fewer* guns (as opposed to the unattainable no guns) will make us safer, if we take into account the threat to our safety posed by the black markets, organized crime, and corruption of law enforcement that would predictably result from a ban on gun ownership. McMahan's prison analogy is therefore entirely irrelevant to the debate.

## Notes

1. In fact, in US law, inmates have no right of self-defence. In *Rowe v. DeBruyn*, 17F.3d 1047 (1994), an inmate used a hotpot to repel an attempted rape. Another inmate came to his aid. All three were disciplined. The inmate who used the hotpot to defend himself argued that he had a right of self-defence. Rather than finding that the hotpot-wielding inmate used excessive force, or that he had no right to use a hotpot in self-defence, the court held that he had no right to self-defence whatsoever.
2. *Collingnon v. Milwaukee Co.*, 163 F.3d 982 (1998); *DeShaney v. Winnebago Co. Dept. of Social Serv.*, 489 U.S. 189 (1989).
3. *Zelig v. County of Los Angeles*, 27 Cal.4th 112 (2002).
4. A scoff-law is a North American term and refers to a person who flouts the law, especially by failing to comply with a law that is difficult to enforce effectively.

# 6

# TRAVEL, FRIENDS, AND KILLING

## Seth Lazar

In early 2015 the British Army Reserves launched a recruitment drive, emphasizing the opportunities that volunteering affords: world travel, professional training, excitement, and comradeship.[1] In this sense it was typical. Military recruitment tends not to mention the possibility of being complicit in murder. But those who are considering a military career know that there is a risk they will be used to fight unjust wars. And killing in unjust wars is arguably little better than murder. How, then, should a morally conscientious individual decide whether to join the armed forces of her state?

First, it obviously depends who you'll be fighting for. Recent years have seen clearly unjust and, at best, dubious wars launched by many of the major military powers (most notably the US and UK in Iraq and Afghanistan, and Russia in South Ossetia and Ukraine). However, even for citizens of those belligerents, the probability that they will be implicated in wrongdoing alone does not settle the matter. Many activities—learning to drive, for example—increase the risk that we will act wrongfully in future; that alone does not render the activity impermissible. We need to know not only the risk of wrongdoing, but also the expectation of good. Whether it is permissible to volunteer depends (at least in part) on whether your expectation of doing good is greater than your expectation of wrongdoing. And of course members of the armed forces do a lot of good. In particular, they provide security to the state they represent, as well as aid to others in need (not only in conflicts).[2]

Working out these expectations for individuals is incredibly challenging. But here is one helpful approach. Start by asking whether the institution is justified. This can mean two things. First, is it morally permissible to have these armed forces, compared with having none at all? Second, are our armed forces the morally best that are feasible in the circumstances? Call the first minimal justification, and the second full justification. One necessary condition of both is that the expectation of good done is greater than the expectation of wrongs caused. Whatever our other moral commitments, if our armed forces are expected to do more wrong than good, relative to having no such institutions, then they cannot be minimally justified; if we expect them to do more wrong than good, relative to alternative feasible institutions, then they cannot be fully justified.

How does the justification of an institution relate to the permissibility of taking part in that institution? Institutions are not made up only by the people who fill their roles. They also have an organizational structure, and they persist through time. But obviously the people in those roles are important parts of the institution. Suppose that the armed forces were fully justified. Then surely participation by at least some of their operatives must be permissible. If the expected good achieved by the institution outweighs the expected bad, then since the institution achieves outcomes only through its members, there must be some whose own contributions realize those values. Perhaps some could be responsible for the lion's share of the good, and others responsible for the bulk of the bad, so that participation by the first group is permissible, but not the second group. But this is unlikely. In warfare the good or bad you do is a function of your causal contribution: those likely to do most good—the people doing the actual fighting, for example, or the generals who direct them—are also those likely to do most wrong.

So, if the institution is fully justified, then the participation that the institution needs in order to function should be permissible, at the individual level. And this means that volunteers are permitted to take the risks of wrongdoing that they take when they join up.

What if the armed forces are only minimally justified? There are two possibilities. On the first, we use the same reasoning as for full justification: the institution cannot be minimally justified if its members are not permitted to perform the roles that the institution depends on for its functioning. So, arguing that volunteering is morally impermissible would amount to arguing that the institutions of the armed forces are not minimally justified.

Secondly, perhaps minimally justified armed forces include roles that are necessary for the institution to function, but are impermissible for those who take them up, because their expectation of wrong is greater than their expectation of good. This might be true of frontline soldiers, for example. To have these justified institutions, perhaps these people must take moral risks that one ought not to take. If minimally justified institutions require that some operatives get dirty hands, then everyone who is able to bear these risks should have an equal prospect of bearing them. It follows that we should endorse conscription. But suppose that some among us volunteer to take on that burden. How should we evaluate their decision? Barring wrongful motivations, and if it is genuinely voluntary, we should surely celebrate it as a remarkable display of not only physical, but moral courage. They are putting both their lives and their souls at risk so that others don't have to, to sustain a minimally justified institution from which we all benefit.

If the armed forces are either minimally or fully justified, then, volunteers are either acting permissibly because the expectation of wrongdoing is outweighed by the expectation of good, or they are heroically running a moral risk that some of us have to run, in order to maintain minimally justified institutions.

The real question, then, is not whether individuals are permitted to join the armed forces, but whether the armed forces themselves are at least minimally justified. Or to put it another way: if you want to argue that joining the military is morally impermissible, you must be prepared to conclude that the military should be disbanded.

## Notes

1. See <http://www.army.mod.uk/news/26868.aspx> Similar themes predominate on the US army recruitment website (which, interestingly, places much more emphasis on patriotic duty), see <http://www.goarmy.com>

2. For example, US military helicopters provided vital aid during the 2015 earthquakes in Nepal: <http://www.abc.net.au/news/2015-05-15/us-helicopter-wreckage-found-by-nepals-army/6473950>

# 7

# THE COURAGEOUS
# SUICIDE BOMBER?

Roger Crisp

S ince the 1980s the frequency of suicide attacks—primarily bombing—
has increased rapidly. There are now hundreds every year. As I write,
the BBC is reporting a suicide bombing which appears to have killed
eight people in Pakistan.[1] The motivation of suicide bombers has been
widely discussed by sociologists, historians, psychologists, and others. My
topic, however, is not their motivation, but their moral status.

It is not uncommon to hear the claim—often from politicians or a
spokesperson of those attacked—that suicide bombers are cowardly.
A representative instance was President Bush's response to the assassination of President Bhutto in Pakistan in which he condemned the
'cowardly act'.[2] Here the thought seems to be that suicide bombing is
the 'easy' way to seek to achieve one's political goals, and that greater
'moral courage' would be shown in a 'fair fight' with opponents or in
sustained peaceful political campaigning over a lifetime.

This view, however, strikes many as absurd. Rather, they argue, even if
the goals and methods of suicide bombers are evil, their actions are in fact
brave or courageous. For they knowingly put themselves in situations of
great danger, for a cause in which they sincerely believe. Courage, then, is
seen as what philosophers have called an 'executive' virtue, one which
enables the agent to pursue any dangerous goal, whether good or bad.

But I think this view is also problematic. For a virtue is a good quality
to have, and demands our admiration. How can it be possible that we
are required to admire someone for the way they pursue evil ends?

In the last few decades philosophers have thought hard about the
virtues, and the philosopher whom they most often cite as an authority

is Aristotle.[3] Aristotle's view provides a solution to our question of whether suicide bombers are cowardly or courageous. According to him, they are neither. Aristotle sees that human lives can be understood as consisting in certain 'spheres', and that within each sphere what is important, morally speaking, is living—and in particular acting and feeling—as one ought. Take the emotions, for example, and in particular the emotion of anger. All of us are prone to anger on certain occasions. And there are, in a sense, two 'directions' in which we can go wrong in this particular sphere. We can feel anger when we shouldn't, at the wrong time, towards the wrong people, for the wrong reasons, and so on (and in doing this we display a vice of 'excess'); or we can *fail* to feel anger when we should, at the right time, towards the right people, for the right reasons, and so on (this will be the 'deficient' vice). Virtuous people will hit what Aristotle calls 'the mean', and will feel anger when they should, at the right time, towards the right people, etc.

This account will work for just about any 'neutrally describable' feeling or action you like, including, of course, fear. Now, the brave person will conquer their fear *only* when they should and for the right reasons. So a suicide bomber, pursuing an evil end by evil means, cannot be brave. Will he or she be cowardly? Well, no, because that consists in not conquering fear when one should. Cowardice is the deficient vice in the sphere of fear. The excessive vice consists in conquering fear when one shouldn't, for the wrong reasons, and so on. Aristotle calls it 'rashness'. Suicide bombers, then, who pursue evil ends through evil means, are neither brave nor cowardly. They are rash and so do not deserve our, or anyone else's, admiration.

But why does it matter what we call suicide bombers? I suppose (like some philosophers) one might just be concerned with understanding the way the moral world is, and making true claims about it. But there is also a more pragmatic reason. How an act is described will have consequences. Part of 'radicalizing' potential suicide bombers involves praising the courage of those who have already acted in the cause. That's going to happen anyway, because the radicalizers, of course, believe that the cause is right. But it would be regrettable if their claims about courage were reinforced by those who didn't believe in that cause. And, to repeat, it just sounds very implausible to say that suicide bombers are cowards. I can imagine that someone may think 'rash' isn't quite the right word; it sounds a bit mild. Would 'zealots' be better? I think not. 'Zealot' is a 'hot', emotional word, while 'rash' is colder and more rational. Fighting emotion with emotion is not the right approach to suicide bombing; rather we should encourage suicide bombers to reflect on what they are doing, to others and to themselves.

# Notes

1. <http://news.bbc.co.uk/1/hi/world/7701435.stm>
2. <http://www.washingtonpost.com/wp-dyn/content/article/2007/12/27/AR2007122700753.html>
3. See especially *Nicomachean Ethics*, book 2, chapter 6; and book 3, chapters 6–9.

# 8

# CHEMICAL WEAPONS

*In defence of double standards*

Owen Schaefer

With the US and other nations grappling with how to respond to the war in Syria, the alleged use of chemical weapons by the Assad regime against civilians has received great attention. Horrific reports of a chemical attack in a Damascus suburb in August 2013 that killed hundreds provided a justification for air strikes against Assad's forces in Syria.[1] Yet, some have argued that this focus on chemical weapons use is inconsistent. Here, for example, are the sardonic comments of Dominic Tierney at *The Atlantic Monthly*: 'Blowing your people up with high explosives is allowable, as is shooting them, or torturing them. But woe betide the Syrian regime if it even thinks about using chemical weapons!'[2]

He has a point, though one that should not be taken too far.

The use of chemical weapons is hardly the only human-rights violation in Syria. Hundreds may have been killed by chemical weapons, but tens of thousands more have been killed in the conflict overall. What's more, Assad's regime was already in clear violation of the Geneva Convention, what with rampant killing and torturing of civilians. Indeed, it was the slaughter of anti-Assad protestors that prompted the internal conflict to begin with. If the Obama administration was really interested in protecting the human rights of the Syrian people with force, he would have intervened long ago. What difference does it make that Assad was perpetrating war crimes with chemical weapons, in addition to conventional weapons?

But it does make a difference. It *is* generally worse to be killed by a chemical weapon than a conventional one. Chemical agents typically cause significant suffering before death—choking, vomiting, chemical burns, defecation, and convulsions. Those who survive may be brain damaged. Conventional weapons are not pleasant either, to be sure. Nevertheless, the suffering is pretty much inevitable in a chemical attack, whereas at least those killed by conventional weapons may be killed quickly, even instantly. What's more, chemical weapons are more dispersive than most conventional weapons, more likely to cause collateral damage to non-combatants. For these reasons we should prefer, if a conflict is going to occur at all, that conventional rather than chemical weapons be used.

The critic will argue that these differences are relatively trivial. A more painful or less discriminatory attack is inconsequential in light of the bigger issue: the massive atrocities carried out in Syria.

But that does not make the distinction between chemical and conventional weapons irrelevant. Failing to treat chemical weapons attacks as a separate and more grievous category in warfare would be a serious mistake.

Consider three policy alternatives:

1) Countries treat chemical weapons and conventional weapons as roughly equivalent, and categorically ban both types. This has the virtue of consistency and simplicity, but it's overly pacifistic—no just wars could be fought. Also, enforcing a ban on all weapons on belligerent regimes would be extremely difficult, probably impossible, especially as conventional weapons could not be used to enforce the ban.

2) Countries treat chemical and conventional weapons as roughly equivalent, and categorically ban neither. This again has the virtue of consistency. But, it seems overly permissive: chemical weapons will be employed by various sides in internal and international conflicts, leading to far more suffering.

3) Countries categorically ban chemical weapons, but do not categorically ban conventional weapons. This is roughly the current international regime, and strikes me as an appropriate compromise (though some conventional weapons are indeed also banned, such as land mines). The compromise allows countries to pursue just wars while providing some limitation on the suffering and collateral damage they can impose. What's more, it provides a

disincentive to even those fighting unjust wars: if the use of chemical weapons is more likely to prompt an international intervention in an otherwise internal or regional conflict, various actors have a reason to avoid their use.

So, at least in some circumstances, the use of chemical weapons may well be an appropriate trigger for international humanitarian intervention. Although the focus on chemical weapons may smack of inconsistency, given other grievous human-rights violations already occurring, it is perfectly fair to treat the chemical weapons attack by Assad's forces as a particularly grievous crime that provides a strong reason for intervention.

Postscript: The above was written in the early stages of the Syrian civil war. The war later became more complicated, with the US and its allies bombing one of Assad's strongest enemies, the Islamic State of Iraq and Syria (ISIS), and Russia bombing both ISIS and US-backed rebels. Indeed, the earlier proposed bombing campaign against Assad's forces might well have emboldened ISIS, facilitating atrocities even worse than the chemical weapons attacks perpetrated by Assad's forces. So, whether such a campaign would have been, all-things-considered, justified remains an open question. Still, in the face of bombing threats, Assad's government did agree to abide by international treaties and dismantle its chemical weapons stockpile; international airstrikes against his regime were then averted, and a large quantity of Syrian chemical weapons were destroyed. This is just the sort of outcome one would want from the threat of international force: compliance (admittedly not total) without actual use of force.

## Notes

1. <http://www.theguardian.com/world/middle-east-live/2013/aug/26/syria-crisis-military-action-un-inspectors-vist-chemical-attack> <http://www.bbc.co.uk/news/world-middle-east-23777201>
2. <http://www.theatlantic.com/international/archive/2012/12/syrian-civilians-better-hope-they-die-in-the-right-way/265848/>

# 9

# LOOTED ARTWORKS

*A portrait of justice*

Cécile Fabre

In 1999 Maria Altman, who had fled Austria in 1938 following the Anschluss with Germany, filed a lawsuit against the Austrian government. Her claim was that five paintings by Gustav Klimt had been looted by the Nazis from her uncle before falling into the possession of the Austrian authorities, and that these ought to be returned to her as the rightful heir. Two of the paintings included portraits of her aunt, such as the famous *Woman in Gold*. The Austrians initially refused to take her request seriously, but eventually gave in after several dramatic legal twists and turns.[1]

This story is now on our cinema screens under the title *A Woman in Gold*, with Helen Mirren in the starring role. The ending is clearly meant to be regarded as a happy one: after all, Altman does get the paintings back. And, generally, many think that stolen or plundered works of art ought to be returned to those from whom they were taken, or their heirs.

I do not think that those legal claims are supported by what I and other cosmopolitans regard as a plausible theory of justice, whereby all individuals, wherever they reside in the world, have rights to the resources needed for a flourishing life, and hold those rights not just against their compatriots but also against well-off distant strangers. At the bar of justice, the well-off are under obligations to do far more than they are currently doing; obligations that they could and should discharge by paying more taxes both on what they currently earn and own, and on what they receive from their forebears. The theory also implies that extant property holdings are unjust, resulting as they do from past generations' failure to meet their obligations of justice.

So what about restitutive claims made by the heirs of those who had artwork dispossessed by the Nazis? Those claims are often blocked on the grounds that claimants would not exist but for the fact that their ancestors were wronged. A refugee from the Nazis, who subsequently had children, would not have had these very same children had this upheaval in their life not have occurred. Interestingly, the objection is unlikely to work for all claimants in the case of looted artwork. Some heirs (indeed, Altman herself) were already born then. And even when it is true of some claimants that they would not exist but for the war during which the looting took place, it is not plausible to say that none of them would exist *but for the act of looting itself.*

And yet there are good reasons, grounded in considerations of justice, for resisting those restitutive claims. For under no plausible description of the world as it stood in 1939 can it be held that it was a just world; a world, that is, where all individuals, wherever they reside, enjoyed the basic necessities of life. To bring about a just world *then* would have required heavier taxation and considerably more stringent restrictions on inheritance than were in fact imposed. The wealthy—those who were able to acquire (or commission) paintings—did not have a legitimate title to their monetary resources and thus did not have a legitimate title to what they acquired with those resources (any more than I have a morally legitimate title to a painting I buy thanks to money I have stolen from you). If the war-time possessor was not in fact the painting's rightful owner, nor are his heirs. Moreover, *even if* he was the rightful owner, there are reasons to doubt that his heirs are. For under no plausible description of the world as it has stood since 1939 may we say that it has been a just world, for exactly the same reasons as given above.

The general point, then, is this: there are very good, justice-based reasons to think that the descendants of those from whom those objects were taken are not the rightful owners of those artefacts. Importantly, it does not follow that looters' descendants are entitled to hold on to those objects. For the claim that someone is not the rightful owner of a good *g* does not imply that *g* may be forcibly taken away from him, or withheld from him, by whomever so wishes: Austrian and German combatants who, either acting individually in a private capacity or collectively under the authority of their leadership, forcibly seized enemy property, wrongfully held on to those resources instead of using them to bring about a just, or less unjust, world. In so far as they clearly were not those objects' rightful owners, nor are their descendants.

What, then, are we to do?

It seems to me that there are two different solutions to this problem. On the one hand, one could envisage a global redistribution of stolen artworks away from the art-rich towards the art-poor. Of the five paintings at the heart of Altman's case, one was bought for $135 million by the Neue Gallery in Manhattan with the help of a wealthy philanthropist, and the others were bought by private collectors. But Manhattan is awash with great art; many places around the world are not. Access to art is (I believe) a component of a flourishing life; moreover, evidence suggests that engagement with the arts contributes to improving the socio-economic prospects of deprived populations.[2] The cash donation and the painting could have been put to better use, from the point of view of justice.

On the other hand, one could also envisage a system whereby artefacts that have been wrongfully taken away from a wrongful *de facto* possessor are sold to the highest bidder, with the proceeds to go either to the relief of worldwide poverty or to a global reparations and reconstruction fund for countries torn by war. Although access to art is important in the ways just suggested, access to the basic necessities of life is more urgent, which suggests that the latter solution is to be preferred to the former, so long as there still are individuals in the world who are dying of thirst and starvation. The other four paintings were sold to private collectors. We are told at the end of *A Woman in Gold* that Maria Altman donated the proceeds of the sale to (inter alia) various charities. At the bar of justice, one can only applaud. But overall, as a paradigm example of what ought to be done with stolen artworks—return them to their original legal owners, for them to do as they wish—I am not convinced at all that *A Woman in Gold* does have a happy ending.

## Notes

1. See <http://www.nytimes.com/2011/02/09/arts/design/09altmann.html?_r=0> for details of the case.
2. See, e.g., <http://borgenproject.org/5-ways-art-can-help-alleviate-poverty/>

# HEALTH AND MEDICINE

# 10

# HOMEOPATHY

*An undiluted proposal*

Steve Clarke

The Australian National Health and Medical Research Council[1] has recently conducted a comprehensive review of evidence about homeopathy, hailed as the most thorough evaluation of homeopathy ever conducted.[2] It confirms what has already been established by every major scientific study of homeopathy. There is no evidence that homeopathic remedies are effective other than as placebos. So it is irrational to use homeopathic remedies in preference to medical treatments that have been proven to work.

The ineffectiveness of homeopathy should be of no surprise to anyone with a basic scientific education, but, nevertheless, government health agencies in a number of countries—including France, Denmark, and the UK—continue to subsidize, or cover the full costs, of homeopathic remedies. Which raises a simple question: why do they do this?

In some cases, the answer may be because key people in the relevant government agencies believe that homeopathic remedies work, despite the overwhelming evidence to the contrary. However, others defend the decision to pay for homeopathy by stressing the importance of patient choice. In 2010 the UK's National Health Service (NHS) issued a statement conceding that there was no evidence that homeopathic remedies work, but appealing to patient choice to justify paying for homeopathy (subject to the recommendation of local doctors).[3] The NHS's basic line of argument is anti-paternalist. People should have the option to be irrational if they wish, providing they are not harming others. What is important is that people are supplied with all information relevant to their decision-making. It is not the state's role to prevent people from making foolish choices.

Even if we accept this argument, however, the state also has a duty to limit its demands on taxpayers. In circumstances where the use of homeopathic remedies is actually cheaper than conventional medical alternatives, the state should be willing to pay for, or subsidize, the use of homeopathic remedies, so as to save money. The savings could then be used to pay for conventional medical treatments that work, or for some other good purpose, or returned to taxpayers.

The NHS statement noted that the organization spends between £3 million and £4 million per year on approximately 25,000 homeopathic items. That is an average of between £120 and £160 per item. Presumably much of this money is spent on staff costs and only some of it on homeopathic remedies, which are offered to patients in the form of pills, ointments, gels, crystals, and small dropper bottles of extremely diluted liquid.

But the NHS has a responsibility to spend the money in its budget wisely. If, for example, there is a choice of two homeopathic remedies that are available, each of which is equally effective, then the NHS should fund the cheapest of these only. Similarly, if there are two homeopaths available to provide a homeopathic remedy, then the NHS should only agree to employ the cheapest of these. To do otherwise is to throw away money needlessly.

Since the NHS concedes that there is no evidence that homeopathic remedies actually work, it implicitly also concedes that there is no evidence that homeopathic training makes any difference to the efficacy of homeopathy. It follows that the NHS should be indifferent to employing either trained or untrained homeopaths. The overriding consideration should be cost. The NHS should employ the cheapest available people willing to act as homeopaths. The NHS should offer the minimum wage to homeopaths. If currently employed NHS homeopaths are unwilling to work for the minimum wage then they should be replaced by members of the currently unemployed who are willing to do so.

Similarly, the NHS should save all that it can on the costs of acquiring homeopathic remedies. These remedies must be extremely cheap to manufacture in bulk, given that they are created by diluting an active substance in vast quantities of water. If suppliers cannot be found who can produce homeopathic remedies at competitive prices, then the NHS should make its own homeopathic remedies. The NHS is right to support patient choice, but it is outrageous that millions of pounds are spent on homeopathy each year when a similarly effective service could be provided to patients at a small fraction of this cost.

## Notes

1. National Health and Medical Research Council (5 March 2015). *Homeopathy Review* <https://www.nhmrc.gov.au/health-topics/complementary-medicines/homeopathy-review>
2. Ernst, E. (12 March 2015). 'There is no scientific case for homeopathy: the debate is over', *The Guardian* <http://www.theguardian.com/commentisfree/2015/mar/12/no-scientific-case-homeopathy-remedies-pharmacists-placebos>
3. National Health Service (27 July 2010). 'Homeopathy remains on the NHS', *NHS News.* <http://www.nhs.uk/news/2010/July07/Pages/nhs-homeopathy.aspx>

# 11

# FIVE MINUTES TOO LATE

## Lachlan de Crespigny and Julian Savulescu

Windsor Coroner's Court has heard that Claire Teague died within hours of giving birth at home after a private midwife committed a horrifying catalogue of errors.[1] A coroner ruled that there were 'missed opportunities' to save Claire.[2]

The midwife seems to have prioritized homebirth over life itself.[3] 'Claire had a great pregnancy,' she was quoted as saying, 'she had a really lovely spontaneous birth at home and I hope [her husband] Simon in time will remember that.'

This case involved the death of the mother. But the mother's health is not all that's at stake, of course.

Preventable serious disabilities are inevitable after some homebirths. Take the case of Bizzie. Her baby, Sarai, was breech—something which had been undiagnosed in labour.[4] The midwife had difficulty delivering her head, and she was unresponsive at birth. Sarai required 15 minutes' resuscitation. She was flown to a neonatal intensive care unit, but was having seizures every 20 minutes. She is now severely handicapped and wheelchair-bound.

Homebirth perinatal deaths of infants who would have survived if they had been born in hospital are more common than maternal deaths.[5] Professionals and pregnant women have an ethical obligation to minimize risk of long-term harm to the future child. Consistent with this, antenatal care focuses on minimizing the risk of harm to the future child, such as by advocating alcohol abstinence in pregnancy, folic acid supplementation to reduce the chance of neural tube defect, and minimizing teratogenic risks of medications in pregnancy (teratogens may cause birth defects).

Currently the homebirth debate focuses on the headline disasters, such as Claire Teague's. Yet the silent tragedies are not the deaths. They are the long-term disabilities that result from homebirth.

Homebirth can cause a delay in diagnosis, delivery, and/or transfer following an acute event (like compromise of blood flow to the baby's brain) during delivery with rapidly developing asphyxia. When the oxygen supply to the brain is compromised, seconds matter. But transfer from home to proper resuscitation facilities takes minutes, sometimes many minutes. That can result in permanent severe intellectual disability or quadriplegia.

Good data are not available on the risk of long-term disability after homebirth. Large long-term follow-up studies are desperately needed.[6] But what risk of quadriplegia should a parent take to have a homebirth? One in a thousand? One in a million?

Maternal autonomy includes the right for mothers to risk their own death. But we contend that the choice to have 'a really lovely spontaneous birth at home' is only justified if it exposes the future child to zero risk of avoidable disability. And this is just never the case.

People often respond that, in routine pregnancies, the additional risk of a homebirth is tiny. Some claim that the value of birth at home (for example, to the mother–child bond) outweighs that small chance of a catastrophic event.

We disagree. Having a homebirth is like failing to buckle up your child when you drive. The probability of being injured in a single trip by not wearing a seat belt is extremely low. Still, we expect people to wear a seat belt to make the risk as low as possible, despite some inconvenience and diminution of driving pleasure. Wearing a seat belt won't remove all risk of injury or death. Indeed, on rare occasions, it might even cause greater injury. But on balance it is much safer with a seat belt. And if one child is permanently brain damaged because she did not wear a seat belt, that is one child too many.

## Notes

1. Andrew Levy (5 September 2012). 'Inquest told midwife who "brain-washed" woman into having homebirth made a series of errors that led to mother's death'. *Mail Online*. <http://www.dailymail.co.uk/health/article-2198725/

Claire-Teague-death-Wife-bleeds-death-midwife-Rosie-Kacary-persuaded-homebirth.html>

2. *BBC* (6 September 2012). 'Claire Teague: "Missed opportunities" in home birth death'. <http://www.bbc.com/news/uk-england-berkshire-19510075>

3. Adams, Stephen (5 September 2012). 'Mother "brainwashed" over home birth dies'. *The Telegraph.* <http://www.telegraph.co.uk/news/health/news/9523610/Mother-brainwashed-over-home-birth-dies.html>

4. Johnson, S. (28 June 2012). 'Baby died after cord entanglement: coroner'. *Herald Sun.* <http://www.heraldsun.com.au/news/breaking-news/baby-died-after-cord-entanglement-coroner/story-e6frf7kf-1226410986230>

5. Keller, C. (6 June 2012). 'South Australian Coroner wants crackdown on midwives and homebirths'. *The Advertiser.* <http://www.adelaidenow.com.au/news/south-australia/south-australian-coroner-wants-crackdown-on-midwives-and-homebirths/story-e6frea83-1226386012581>

6. de Crespigny, Lachlan and Savulescu, Julian (2014). 'Homebirth and the future child', *Journal of Medical Ethics* 40: 807–12. <http://jme.bmj.com/content/40/12/807?etoc>

## 12

# TAKING DRUGS TO
# HELP OTHERS

## Tom Douglas

Primaquine is an anti-malarial drug. When someone infected with the falciparum malaria parasite takes the drug, it reduces the risk that the parasite will be transmitted to mosquitoes and so to other people. However, it confers no direct benefit on the individual who takes the drug. Indeed it poses a net risk, since it has side effects and can cause a breakdown of red blood cells in certain genetically susceptible individuals. Nevertheless, primaquine is taken as a single dose by millions of people annually.

Triptorelin is a testosterone-suppressing drug that has been used to 'chemically castrate' sex offenders, including paedophiles. It can't redirect misplaced sexual desires, but it can attenuate them, and there is some evidence that this can reduce the risk of recidivism in a subgroup of offenders. Again, though, it can have serious side effects for the user, including depression and softening of the bones.

Both of these drugs, then, can work in ways that benefit third parties, but confer no net benefit on the user of the drug.[1] This has led some to question whether it is ethical to prescribe them, even when the user freely consents to their use.[2] For example, Kevin Baird and Claudia Surjadjaja have argued that prescribing single-dose primaquine for third-party benefit may be ethical in some cases, but only when the risks to the patient fall within certain limits. Measured risks can be taken, but significant risks of serious harm cannot.[3]

The concern here is not that primaquine and triptorelin are being used *in part* for their benefits to third parties. This is the case with many medical interventions, as when an AIDS patient uses anti-retroviral therapy in part to reduce the risk of infecting others. This seems unproblematic. Rather the worry is that, in some cases at least, the use of primaquine and triptorelin may have *no* benefit for the user and indeed may pose a risk of serious harm. It may thus violate the requirement that seriously risky medical interventions should not be provided *solely* to bring about benefits to the third parties, even when their use is voluntary. They should be provided only when they're in the best interests of the individual who undergoes the intervention.

Let us call this the 'best interests requirement'.

The best interests requirement is widely accepted, at least as a rough rule of thumb, both by medical ethicists and medical practitioners (though some might allow an exception for cases in which the third parties are friends or family, as, for example, in cases of sibling-sibling organ donation). But I find it puzzling. It's generally regarded as ethically acceptable for a person to undergo a risky procedure to benefit herself. And surely it's *more* admirable to take a risky drug to benefit others. So why adopt a principle that rules out altruistic treatments while allowing self-interested ones? In many other contexts individuals are encouraged to expose themselves to physical and mental risks for the social good; consider allied efforts to recruit soldiers to fight Nazism during World War II.

Perhaps some think that the best interests requirement is necessary to prevent the misuse of medical technologies. We should accept the requirement since, if we do not, we are likely to subsequently accept seriously immoral uses of medicine to benefit society. Although the consensual provision of risky but socially beneficial medical interventions might be ethically acceptable taken in isolation, we have no way of enabling this without also creating a risk of more extreme, ethically objectionable practices. So we should adopt a moral requirement that rules out all seriously risky interventions that are not in the interests of the user.

This rationale looks superficially persuasive. Humanity does have a bad track record of coercively and misguidedly adopting intrusive and risky medical interventions perceived to have social benefits: think of the past use of frontal lobotomy to control putatively anti-social behaviour and of coercive sterilization to achieve the social benefit of better genes for future generations.

However, it's at least open to question whether concerns about past misuse are sufficiently powerful to justify forgoing the social benefits of interventions like single-dose primaquine and triptorelin-induced chemical castration.

In the wake of diabolical attempts to achieve social goals through medicine in the twentieth century, it may have been reasonable to introduce a strict best interests requirement. But we have since made a good deal of progress in medical ethics; the risk of serious misuse is much lower than before, at least in countries that witnessed a 'medical ethics revolution' in the late twentieth century. And we've acquired greater technological capacity to achieve genuine social benefits through medicine. It's now time to rethink the requirement.

## Notes

1. Vaccines also sometimes share these features when they are used in individuals who stand to benefit little from the vaccination, but whose vaccination will help to confer herd immunity on the population.
2. See Grubin, D. and Beech, A. (2010). 'Chemical castration for sex offenders', *British Medical Journal* 340: 433–4, at p. 434.
3. Baird, J.K. and Surjadjaja, C. (2011). 'Consideration of ethics in primaquine therapy against malaria transmission', *Trends in Parasitology* 27/1: 11–16, at p. 15.

# 13

# MY SON'S DYSLEXIC, AND I'M GLAD

Charles Foster

My son is dyslexic, and I'm glad.

Most people think that I am deranged or callous. But I have two related reasons, both of which seem to me to be good.

The first is that his dyslexia is an inextricable part of him. I can't say: 'This is the pathological bit, which I resent', as one might say of a tumour. Take away his dyslexia and he wouldn't be the same person, but able to read and write. He wouldn't be him. That would be far too high a price for me to pay. And for him to pay? Well, there you run into Parfit's non-identity problem. I would have a child without dyslexia, but I wouldn't have *that* child.[1] If my son un-wished his dyslexia, he'd un-wish himself.

The second is that I can't bring myself to say that his dyslexia is pathological. To use the old, deeply inaccurate language of brain lateralization, he's a right-brain person. He sees holistically; he's a big picture person; he intuits; he connects wildly distant and different concepts. There's a cost, of course. There always is. His left brain doesn't do as well with the boring, nerdish, reductionist, systematic, literal things that our world sees as the essential elements of education. But surely he's the real intellectual aristocrat, if only we could define 'intellectual' in a way that isn't dictated purely by that self-serving left side.[2] If you could choose between being literal and being literary, would you opt to be literal?

Of course I'm romanticizing dyslexia, and putting on a brave face for him and for me. There will be great struggles and frustrations. But let's be clear why that is. It's because the educational system, and the world of work beyond it, sees everything from its own left-brain perspective. It will try to turn him into a left-brainer, whether he likes it or not, and regardless of the value of the right-brain stuff.

So here's the relevance of this personal story to a philosophy book. Our values are overwhelmingly, crushingly conditioned by the presumption that it is good to be regular, systematic, ordered, and literal. Anything else is diseased, and the diseased want to be cured, don't they? So dyslexics are compulsorily treated. They have educational therapy forcibly administered to them against their will for years.

It can be put in yet another pejorative, quasi-legal way. There is systematic discrimination against right-brain dominance, of a sort that would be regarded as outrageous were it directed against skin colour rather than neuronal wiring.

What's to be done? So far as the changing of attitudes is concerned, there's perhaps some value in diatribes, like the one above, using the explosive language of discrimination.

The wrongness of discrimination can be described in many ways. But the way that is most apposite here is that it entails inflicting a harm on the discriminator, not the discriminatee. It's a classic example of self-harming. Mountfield and Singh observed that 'dignity is Janus-faced':[3] if X sets out to degrade Y, the main casualty is almost always X, not Y. To deny and decry otherness is to be alone; to deny and decry variety is to be insensate; to deny and decry the whole is to be achingly parochial. None is consistent with human thriving.

This doesn't mean that I don't acknowledge that there is such a thing as pathology. There is. There is a moral point to at least some medicine. But I am confused about where the boundary between pathology and gift lies, and hence about the legitimate scope of therapeutic adventure. I don't know whether to give growth hormone to a child with achondroplasia—because it will change the person fundamentally—is tantamount to murder. I would be even less sure about the propriety of a chemical cure of an adult achondroplastic. I am correspondingly agnostic about the relevance of the 'patient's' own wishes about 'cure' where her case lies close to that mysterious border. But I am clear that, wherever the border lies, my gleefully anarchic, iconoclastic son—who snaps up the world in one mouthful and knows how the *whole thing* explodes on the palate—lives, for the moment, in the heart of the capital of Gift-Land.

As for us? Well, we'll hypocritically and shabbily compromise with the zeitgeist, I suppose, which means continuing to torment our son with flashcards and phonemes when he's actually thinking far bigger thoughts than any we could imagine. We'll collaborate with the left-brain establishment that demands his acquiescence. But we'll always wonder what we, and he, have lost.

## Notes

1. For an accessible account of the non-identity problem, see <http://plato. stanford.edu/entries/nonidentity-problem/>
2. See McGilchrist, Iain (2009). *The Master and His Emissary: The Divided Brain and the Making of the Western World* (New Haven, CT: Yale University Press).
3. Mountfield, Helen and Singh, Rabinder (January 2004). 'The value of dignity'. Paper presented to British-Israeli Legal Exchange, London.

# 14

# THE POINT OF DEATH

Janet Radcliffe Richards

*The Guardian* reported the death of the man who had been so tragically shot in Antigua, with his wife, three weeks after their wedding.[1] The report began like this:

> Ben Mullany, the newlywed who was shot on honeymoon in Antigua in an attack that killed his wife, Catherine, died in hospital in Wales yesterday after his life support machine was switched off. The 31-year-old trainee physiotherapist, who had suffered a fractured skull and had a bullet lodged in the back of his head, was flown back to Britain while in a coma on Saturday. Tests carried out when his condition stabilised after the 24-hour journey established he was brain dead.

This is a familiar way of describing such happenings, even among clinical professionals. Brain death is pronounced, so the life support machine is switched off, and the patient dies. The clear implication is that brain death is not death. The machine is still keeping the patient alive, and it is switching off the machine that causes real death.

This was not the intention of the people who introduced the concept of brain death. Their intention was to offer an alternative means of diagnosing death as such. For a very long time doctors had used the cardiopulmonary criterion (cessation of breathing and heartbeat) to establish death, but the development of the mechanical ventilator ('life support machine') meant that many patients whose brains were no longer functioning, and who had no chance whatever of recovering either consciousness or spontaneous breathing, were still, by these criteria, alive. This caused many difficulties. These were particularly acute for the developing transplantation programme, which needed donors that were dead, but organs that were kept fresh by the ventilator. But it had wider implications of many kinds, such as in the enormous cost of keeping people on ventilators in intensive care when there was no chance of their ever recovering.

So it was proposed in 1967, and has since been widely accepted, that brain death should be accepted as a criterion for death as such. But, of course, by the original cardiopulmonary criterion, ventilated brain-dead bodies should still count as alive—as in many parts of the world, and to a considerable extent in both popular and medical intuition, they still do. Which of these views about death, and the variations on them, is right?

This fundamentally important point is that this problem is not one that can possibly be solved by science or technology. Science can tell us, with increasing accuracy, what state any body is in, and what chance there is for reversal of any declining function. But that does not amount to telling us which of those states is really death.

This is true whatever you think death actually is. If, as many people believe, the essence of life is the presence of an immaterial soul, death occurs when that soul finally leaves the body; but as science cannot detect souls, it cannot determine when that is. If, on the other hand, life is a complex organization of physical parts and nothing further, then when you know everything there is to know about the physical state of the body, you know everything there is to know. There simply is no further, objective question of whether the person is really dead. Some parts or aspects may be dead while others continue, and the question is which we are going to count as constituting overall death.

Either way, then, the question of when death occurs is not a scientific one; this means the problem needs to be understood in a different way. The reason why the diagnosis of death has mattered so much is that the difference between life and death is traditionally of enormous *moral* importance, and the problem we are faced with now must be recognized as a moral one. Rather than a decision about the true moment of death, we need a decision about the *morally appropriate treatment* of people at the different stages of the closing-down process that everyone recognizes as dying.

To people who think there is an objective point of death, even though we cannot be sure when it occurs, it may seem that the only acceptable course is the traditional one of waiting until there can be no possible doubt. To those who think there is no more to human life than a complex arrangement of physical parts, however, the problem is to determine which aspects of the individual are the ones that are morally significant. The proposal of the brain death criterion depended on the idea that what mattered was personhood. The idea was that when brain function had finally gone, along with consciousness and all that went with it, the ventilator was pumping blood around an empty shell rather than a person.

But although the brain death criterion is now widely accepted, the personhood idea makes the life/death distinction very uncomfortable around the margins, because by that standard people should probably be declared dead when their upper brains are so damaged as to preclude any possibility of consciousness or its return, even though the brain stem is still intact and spontaneous breathing continues. (This is the case with many patients in the state known as PVS, 'persistent vegetative state', who are still counted as alive and who can be maintained for many years by artificial feeding.)

All this raises serious doubts about whether we should recognize a sudden change of moral status between life and death at all. Perhaps there needs to be a penumbral morality, to go with the penumbral states between the clearly alive and the clearly dead—before what is clearly death, but after the individual's interests have finally gone.

From the press reports, it sounds as though it was clear soon after the shooting that Mr Mullany's brain had been comprehensively and irretrievably damaged, and that there was no chance of his ever becoming the same person—or any person—again. This seems to have been recognized even before he was declared (brain) dead, and before his being returned to the UK for continued treatment. His continuation on the ventilator did him no harm, but it did him no good either. It gave his parents some kind of hope because he had not actually been declared dead—but hope of what? Was it morally worthwhile to devote enormous amounts of skill and money to maintain his circulation and other bodily functions while flying him back to the UK? Doing so was a natural and understandable response to a great tragedy, but was it the right one?

Given the ever increasing powers of technology to keep some parts and aspects of the body functioning when others have been irretrievably lost, and given the colossal expense involved in making use of this technology, it is morally essential to recognize these questions of life and death for what they are. But it will be very difficult to dislodge the idea that we must make a sharp moral dividing line between life and death.

# Note

1. <http://www.guardian.co.uk/world/2008/aug/04/internationalcrime>

# 15

# IS IT ETHICAL TO USE DATA FROM NAZI MEDICAL EXPERIMENTS?

Lynn Gillam

During World War II, Nazi doctors had unfettered access to human beings they could use in medical experiments in any way they chose. In one way, these experiments were just another form of mass torture and murder, so our moral judgement of them is clear. But they also pose an uncomfortable moral challenge: what if some of the medical experiments yielded scientifically sound data that could be put to good use? Would it be justifiable to use that knowledge?

## Using data

It is tempting to deflect the question by saying the data is useless—that the bad behaviour must have produced bad science—so we don't even have to think about it. But there is no inevitable link between the two because science is not a moral endeavour. If scientific data is too poor to use, it is because of poor study design and analysis, not because of the bad moral character of the scientist. And in fact, some of the data from Nazi experiments is scientifically sound enough to be useful.

The hypothermia experiments in which people were immersed in ice water until they became unconscious (and many died), for instance, established the rate of cooling of humans in cold water and provided information about when re-warming might be successful. Data from the Nazi experiments was cited in scientific papers from the 1950s to the 1980s,[1] but with no indication of its nature.

The original source appears as a paper by Leo Alexander, published in Combined Intelligence Objectives Subcommittee Files. This is an unusual type of publication to be mentioned in a scientific journal, and it is unclear that it comes from the trial of Nazi doctors at Nuremberg.[2]

In the late 1980s US researcher Robert Pozos[3] argued the Nazi hypothermia data was critical to improving methods of reviving people rescued from freezing water after boat accidents, but the *New England Journal of Medicine* rejected his proposal to publish the data openly.

Use of data generated by the Nazis from the deadly phosgene gas experiments has also been considered and rejected[4] by the US Environmental Protection Agency, even though it could have helped save lives of those accidentally exposed.

## A tricky conundrum

So should the results of Nazi experiments ever be taken up and used? A simple utilitarian response would look to the obvious consequences. If good can come to people now and in the future from using the data, then its use is surely justified. After all, no further harm can be done to those who died.

But a more sophisticated utilitarian would think about the indirect and subtle consequences. Perhaps family members of those who were experimented on would be distressed to know the data was being used. And their distress might outweigh the good that could be done. Or perhaps using the data would send the message that the experiments weren't so bad after all, and even encourage morally blinkered doctors to do their own unethical experiments.

Of course, these bad consequences could be avoided simply by making sure the data is used in secret, never entering the published academic literature. But recommending deception to solve a moral problem is clearly problematic in itself.

The trouble is that focusing on the consequences—whether good or bad—of using Nazi data, misses an important point: there is a principle at stake here. Even if some good could come of using the data, it would just not be right to use it. It would somehow deny or downplay the evil of what was done in the experiments that generated them.

This is a common sentiment, but, if it is to hold ethical weight, we need to be able to spell it out and give it a solid foundation. A little reflection shows that, as a society, we don't have an absolute objection to deriving some good out of something bad or wrong. Murder victims sometimes become organ donors, for instance, and there is no concern over whether that is inappropriate.

## Paying our debt

So how to decide when it's all right to derive some good from a wrongdoing? I think the answer lies in considering what society owes ethically to the victims of a wrongdoing. The ongoing investigations into institutional child sexual abuse in a number of Western countries have brought this question sharply into focus.

The wrongs done to victims of abuse are over, but that's not the end of the matter. Victims are ethically owed many things: recognition that what was done to them was indeed wrong; a credible indication that society takes this seriously; an effort to identify, apprehend, and punish the perpetrators; and compensation for their ongoing suffering and disadvantage. But beyond this, we have an obligation not to forget, and not to whitewash.

Victims of Nazi medical experiments are owed these same things. If society's obligations to them have broadly been met through the Nuremberg trials and the ongoing global abhorrence of the awful things done to people in World War II, then it might be ethically possible to use the data if it could lead to some good. But this must only be done with absolute openness about the source of the data, and clear condemnation of the way it was obtained. Citation of the Nazi hypothermia data in the medical and scientific literature from the 1950s to the 1980s gives no hint at all of what is being referred to, and so it falls ethically short.[5]

## Notes

1. <http://onlinelibrary.wiley.com/doi/10.2307/3561733/abstract>
2. <http://jama.jamanetwork.com/article.aspx?articleid=1157153>
3. <http://articles.latimes.com/1988-10-30/news/mn-958_1_nazi-data-issue>
4. <https://www.jewishvirtuallibrary.org/jsource/Judaism/naziexp.html#2>
5. This article was cross-posted on *The Conversation* <https://theconversation.com/uk> We are grateful to *The Conversation* for permission to reproduce.

# 16

# FINANCIAL INCENTIVES, COERCION, AND PSYCHOSIS

Jonathan Pugh

Should sufferers of schizophrenia be paid to take their medication? A contentious report, a few years ago, called on doctors to do just that.[1] The issue has been reignited by an editorial in the *British Medical Journal*.[2] The author describes a recent study that suggests that modest financial incentives can significantly improve adherence in people treated for schizophrenia and other psychoses in the UK.[3]

Some have objected that the practice amounts to coercion; I disagree.

As the editorial points out, it is difficult to achieve adherence to anti-psychotic drugs, because many patients suffering from psychotic disorders do not accept that they are ill, and many anti-psychotic drugs, although highly effective, are associated with unpleasant side effects. The article suggests that offering financial incentives to patients suffering from schizophrenia, in order to achieve adherence, may be morally permissible. However, Joanne Shaw, the former vice chair of NHS Direct, has argued that that practice is coercive, and invalidates the patient's consent. 'Paying people to take medicines sends a signal that they need to be compensated for doing something that is not inherently in their own interests. It is coercion by carrot rather than stick, but coercion nonetheless.'[4]

But is this practice really coercive? I think not. Consider a clear case of coercion: imagine a patient is suffering from a broken shoulder, and competently refuses to consent to what his physician believes is a necessary surgery. Suppose the physician threatens to refuse the patient any further pain relief until he agrees to consent to the operation. Part of what seems problematic here is that the physician seems to undermine the patient's autonomy. The threat is understood to invalidate the patient's consent, because the physician has overridden the patient's will by unduly reducing his options in order to achieve the outcome that the physician believes is best.

This is an example of a coercive threat, and it is uncontroversial to suppose that such threats can invalidate the patient's consent.

But can there be coercion by carrot as well as by stick?

This is much more problematic. Whilst credible conditional threats take away the victim's belief that they are free to maintain the status quo, conditional offers will typically leave the status quo option intact; the recipient may simply refuse the offer. Accordingly, whilst threats serve to subtract a desirable option from the victim's choice set, namely the status quo option, offers will normally serve to supplement this option with a further one.

Of course, there are some exceptions to this. Some offers may change the status quo situation. This is a common line of objection to allowing people the option of voluntary euthanasia. According to this objection, once you give someone the legal option of voluntary euthanasia, they can no longer simply stay alive *by default* as their status quo; rather, their staying alive becomes the result of their choice. Also, offers can sometimes form a part of a coercive situation: for example, if Jones were to steal Smith's wallet, and then offer to return it only if Smith performed some degrading task. Here though, the offer *per se* is not coercive; what makes the situation coercive is the illicit reduction of freedoms that preceded the offer, and which were put in place in order to make the offer.

So why think that offering financial incentives in order to achieve treatment adherence is coercive? Shaw seems to suggest that such offers send the implicit message that the thing that recipients of the offer are being given an incentive to do is not inherently in their own interests. However, the fact that an offer sends a particular message has no bearing on the recipient's available options. As such, even if we believe that the implicit message can ground a moral objection to the practice of making the offer, this is unrelated to the question of whether the offer is coercive. It might be that adherence to a treatment programme is not in the interests of some of those suffering from psychotic illness (perhaps on the basis that anti-psychotic drugs have unpleasant side effects). Again though, this does not entail that the offer is coercive. It is still possible for patients to reject the financial incentive, and to continue with non-adherence; the financial incentive just makes one of the options more appealing than it was.

Of course, the fact that there is nothing coercive about an offer does not entail that it is moral. Suppose, while carrying a backpack full of water bottles, I stumble across a man dying of thirst and offer him one bottle for £1,000,000. Here, I have given the man an incentive (i.e. a bottle of water) to do something not inherently in his own interests (giving me £1,000,000). But it seems implausible to claim that the man could not autonomously consent to agreeing to this transaction. I have not coerced him, but I have acted immorally by treating him unfairly.

So there may well be plausible objections to offering financial incentives to patients in order to achieve adherence to a treatment programme. But the charge of 'coercion' is not one of them.

# Notes

1. <http://www.dailymail.co.uk/news/article-426173/Call-pay-schizophrenics-medication.html>
2. Kendall, Tim (22 October 2013). 'Paying patients with psychosis to improve adherence,' *British Medical Journal* 347: f5782, doi:10.1136/bmj.f5782.
3. Priebe, Stefan, et al. (7 October 2013). 'Effectiveness of financial incentives to improve adherence to maintenance treatment with antipsychotics: cluster randomised controlled trial,' *British Medical Journal* 347: f5847, doi:10.1136/bmj.f5847.
4. Shaw, Joanne (2 August 2007). 'Is it acceptable for people to be paid to adhere to medication? No,' *British Medical Journal* 335/7613: 233, doi:10.1136/bmj.39286.422639.BE.

# 17

# MR NICKLINSON AND THE RIGHT TO DIE

Julian Savulescu

Tony Nicklinson, 58, from Melksham, Wiltshire, has 'locked-in syndrome' after a stroke in 2005.* He is totally paralysed, unable to move anything other than his eyes. According to the BBC report, he 'is unable to carry out his own suicide'. 'He is seeking legal protection for any doctor who helps him end his life.'[1]

In fact, it is not quite correct that Tony Nicklinson 'is unable to carry out his own suicide'. He could at present refuse to eat food or drink fluids. Hunger strikers do this for political reasons. He could do it for personal reasons. People should not be force-fed against their own autonomous wishes.

Now suppose that Mr Nicklinson did refuse to eat or drink, because he found a life locked-in to be intolerable and wanted to die. He would die in weeks, perhaps less. Given that he would die, he should be given medical treatment to make his last weeks as comfortable as possible—including sedation and analgesia (medication to reduce his suffering). He could even be given such doses that render him unconscious.

Such a process already happens, in the UK, in a slightly different way. In the famous case of Tony Bland, who was permanently unconscious, Law Lords authorized the removal of a feeding tube that was keeping him alive. They, as well as his family and doctors, all judged that continued life was not in his interests.

---

* This chapter was written in March 2012. Tony Nicklinson died in August 2012, just a week after he lost his High Court case to allow doctors to end his life.

The process of withholding or removing artificial feeding from patients as young as newborns to elderly people has been commonplace in medicine in many parts of the world. The Bland judgement made it possible for doctors to cause the death of a patient by removing feeding without being liable for murder. (Interestingly, the legal reasoning was that the act of removing the feeding tube was not an act, it was an omission, and so the removal was not murder. However, if a third party had removed Tony Bland's feeding tube, for reasons of some personal gain, that person would seem to have been guilty of murder.)

Now if doctors, courts, and family members can make a decision that a person's life is no longer worth living and feeding should be stopped, why can't the person him/herself make that decision, and it be respected? Surely the person who has the most right to decide whether life is tolerable is the person who must live that life—in this case, Tony Nicklinson.

So it seems to me that, ethically, Tony Nicklinson should now have the right to die by starvation. And if other patients (like Tony Bland) receive palliative care in the form of analgesia and sedation following decisions made by courts, doctors, and their families, then Tony Nicklinson has an equal right to such palliative care as he dies.

So we have established that Tony Nicklinson has the right to starve himself to death, with medical support. He should also be allowed to stipulate the conditions under which, in the future, he should not be fed. This is called an advance directive. He could stipulate, for example, that if he ever became unable to express himself, he should no longer be fed. He would then die, over a period of weeks, with palliative sedation and hydration.

So Tony Nicklinson does have the capacity, now and in the future, to suicide. And he should not be force-fed. That is a violation of a basic human right.

But what, you might ask, is the difference between Tony Nicklinson dying by starvation, perhaps unconscious, over a period of weeks, and him being given a lethal injection that would kill him in seconds, painlessly? In both cases, he will certainly die. Surely it is more humane, in these circumstances, to give him a lethal injection than to allow him to starve himself to death, if that is what he wants?

This is the argument, of course, from suicide, to assisted suicide, to euthanasia. But if one has a right not to eat, then one has a right to euthanasia, at least in moral terms.

The law would classify such euthanasia as murder. For that reason, it is not performed in the UK. But ethically, if a man such as Tony Nicklinson has the right to refuse to eat any longer because he finds his life intolerable, he has the right to be relieved of the suffering of starvation, quickly and painlessly. He has the right to die, including by euthanasia.

## Note

1. <http://www.bbc.co.uk/news/uk-17336774>

# DRUGS AND ORGANS

# 18

# IN PRAISE OF
# ORGAN-IZED SPORT

Dominic Wilkinson

The BBC reports on a recent organ donation initiative in Brazil.[1] This initiative has led to a 400% increase in the number of heart transplants in a local hospital. The waiting list for organs in the city of Recife reportedly dropped to zero in the first year after introduction of this innovation.

What sort of initiative could lead to such a dramatic increase in organ donation numbers?

Most initiatives to increase organs are associated with ethical controversy. But this initiative has nothing to do with amending consent arrangements. It isn't organ conscription or opt-out (presumed consent) donation. It isn't about increasing the pool of organ donors, for example through donation after cardiac death, elective ventilation, or organ donation euthanasia.[2]

The scheme is simple and (almost) completely unproblematic. Sport Club Recife, one of Brazil's largest football clubs, embarked on a publicity campaign two years ago to encourage its fans to become organ donors. At each home game, a television advertisement is played that encourages those attending to become 'immortal fans'. According to the BBC article, 66,000 people have signed up to become organ donors.

There are several enticing features about this campaign. First, it seems specifically designed to appeal to young, male sports fans. That is important because brain death often occurs as a result of serious injury (for example, car accidents) in otherwise healthy people. Those most likely to have this sort of injury are often young and male. But they are also a group that has traditionally had low rates of signing onto organ registries. Young, otherwise healthy men don't think about their deaths or talk with their family about their wishes in the event of a catastrophic injury. Second, the Sport Club Recife organ donation campaign seems to have changed the public conversation about donation. Signing up to the organ donor registry isn't seen to the fans as an optional extra, or as a form of middle-class altruism. The campaign has managed (apparently successfully) to connect fervent and competitive love for a sporting team with donation. Holding one of the bright red Sports Donor cards with your club's insignia on it is seen as a sign of true loyalty to your team.

I said that the Recife initiative was *almost* unproblematic. (Ethicists can always find problems if they look hard enough.) One quibble is with the nature of some of the messages that have been broadcast in the donation advertisements in Recife. Fans have been encouraged to donate so that their love for their team can 'live on in someone else's body'.

'I promise that your eyes will keep on watching Sport Club Recife,' says one man waiting for a cornea transplant in the television ad made to publicize the campaign.

'I promise that your heart will keep on beating for Sport Club Recife,' says a potential recipient of a transplanted heart.

These messages are, frankly, irrational. They tap into quasi-magical thinking about the nature of consciousness and mortality. The notion of a heart 'beating for the club' after transplantation is linked to folk beliefs about the heart as the focus for emotions or the soul. It's not obvious that individuals persuaded to donate by such mystical and incoherent messages have given informed consent.

Of course organ donation after death is different from decisions about medical interventions during life. We don't currently apply stringent standards of informed consent to donation, nor should we. Organ donation after death is the ultimate in 'easy rescue'.[3] This refers to a situation where we are in a position to aid someone else at minimal or no cost to ourselves. Once we have died, our organs are of no use to us, and will be buried or burned if not donated. In 'easy rescue' situations, there is a moral duty to provide aid. So we should be glad that fans have signed the organ donor registry, whatever has motivated them to do so.

The Recife organ donation campaign should be emulated elsewhere, and clubs in Paris and Barcelona have apparently expressed an interest. But we should not stop there. Other popular sporting contests could take advantage of the huge media exposure and emotional investment in local and national teams. For international competitions like the World Cup or Olympics, broadcasters could donate some airtime in each of the participating countries to their national organ donation organizations. Campaigns of this nature would encourage those who have never thought about organ donation to sign up to donor registries. They can convert organ sceptics into donors. Even more surprisingly, they might turn anti-sport philosophers into football fans.

## Notes

1. Carneiro, J. (1 June 2014). 'How thousands of football fans are helping to save lives', *BBC News* magazine. <http://www.bbc.co.uk/news/magazine-27632527>
2. <http://blog.practicalethics.ox.ac.uk/2012/02/obligatory-ventilation-why-elective-ventilation-should-not-be-elective/> <http://blog.practicalethics.ox.ac.uk/2010/05/organ-donation-euthanasia/>
3. Savulescu, J. (2003). 'Death, us and our bodies: personal reflections', *Journal of Medical Ethics* 29: 127–30.

# 19

# DO WE OWN OUR BODIES?

Janet Radcliffe Richards

There was a sad story recently about a young woman who died unexpectedly at the age of 21.[1] She was on the organ donor register and her own mother was on the waiting list for a kidney donation, but the mother was refused one of the kidneys. Even the transplant coordinator was 'crying her eyes out', but there was apparently no escape. Rules were rules. Cadaveric donations must go impartially and anonymously to the most compatible people at the top of the waiting list, and the authorities decreed that these organs must go to three strangers, whose identity the mother will never even know.

The trouble with technological advance is that it keeps forcing us to make decisions in totally new circumstances. We usually start by trying to stretch existing laws and ethical standards to fit the new situation, and these tend to be unhelpful to the cause of transplantation. The special problems for transplantation arise from the fact that for every recipient there must be a donor. We already have a mass of well-established laws and conventions about how to treat human bodies—both living and dead—and since most of them long pre-date the possibility of using parts of one person's body to replace those of another, it is perhaps not surprising that they tend to get in the way. The rules about cadaveric transplant at present are a curious collection. You have no legal right to decide what happens to your body when you die. You can express preferences, but there are some things the law won't let you do (some years ago a man was prevented from leaving his body as meat for the Battersea Dogs' Home), and your relatives are under no obligation to follow your wishes. If it is known that you do not want to be an organ donor, you now (since the Human Tissue Act[2]) have an absolute right to refuse; but you can't insist on being a donor, even if you are suitable.

Your relatives will in practice still be asked for permission and may refuse. They can also give permission, or refuse it, if you have not expressed any wishes. But if you do become a donor, neither you nor your relatives have any right to say anything about who should get the organs, and transplant teams are not allowed to accept any organs given with conditions attached.[3]

Compare this situation with your wishes about the destination of your other possessions. There are some legal limits to what you can do with certain kinds of property—listed buildings or works of art, for instance—and the government will take a share of your estate if it is big enough. But beyond that, your wishes are absolute. You can leave your property to anyone or anything you like, and neither your relatives nor anyone else can veto your wishes. There is certainly no question of anyone's insisting that unless you agree to giving your property to whoever is in most need, it will simply be destroyed—which is what happens to cadaveric organs unless you agree to their being distributed in the established way.

But, it will be said, bodies and body parts are not property, so of course they shouldn't be treated like other things. It's true that, at present, bodies are not property in law, but the interesting question is whether they should be. It is easy, in general terms, to understand why they are not: common law developed from Church law, and traditional Christianity literally anticipated the resurrection of the body at the Last Judgement—as the creeds still attest. Anyway, bodies were of no use to anyone else until scientific anatomy developed, so there was no reason to regard them as property.

But this is something that needs rethinking in the light of technological development. Some body parts and fluids were always of use to other people (hair, teeth, milk) and transferred like other property; now the scope for using body parts, and even detaching them from living people for use elsewhere, is increasing all the time. Laws are being made to control the new possibilities, and they are giving us more and more control over what happens to our bodies, making them seem more and more like our other possessions. Shouldn't they be treated just like other possessions?

Even if it is claimed that we should not go quite that far, we still need to think about why we treat body parts as so different from other things. It may sound good to give cadaveric transplant organs simply to the person 'in most need', but then why not extend the principle to other goods we have to bequeath? How does the required impartiality of cadaveric donation square with the fact that living donations are nearly all directed, and indeed usually expected to be so? And can there be any justification for allowing cadaveric organs to be wasted—and lives lost—rather than accepted on specific conditions?

The curious status of the body is being used as an excuse for all kinds of ill-thought-out, ad hoc policies, which have no more coherent moral underpinning than the immediate intuitions of the people making the rules. Technology is all the time increasing the ways in which bodies and body parts really are like other things we own. Matching this with a recognition of them as property in law would be a useful step in the direction of clear thinking about these issues.

# Notes

1. <http://news.bbc.co.uk/1/hi/england/bradford/7344205.stm>
2. <http://www.opsi.gov.uk/ACTS/acts2004/ukpga_20040030_en_1>
3. <http://www.uktransplant.org.uk/ukt/newsroom/statements_and_stances/statements/directed_donation.jsp>

# 20

# PSYCHIATRIC DRUGS AND
# RELIGIOUS NORMS

Katrien Devolder

Psychiatric drugs are reportedly used frequently within Israel's Haredi community in order to help members conform to religious norms.[1] Haredi Judaism is the most conservative form of Orthodox Judaism. It is sometimes referred to by outsiders as ultra-Orthodox. Haredim typically live in communities that have limited contact with the outside world. Their lives revolve around Torah study, prayer, and family.

In December 2011 the Israel Psychiatric Association held a symposium entitled 'The Haredi Community as a Consumer of Mental-Health Services'. One of the speakers was Professor Omer Bonne, director of the psychiatry department at Hadassah University Hospital. Professor Bonne said that sometimes students at yeshiva, a religious school, and married men should be given antidepressants even if they do not suffer from depression, because these drugs also suppress sex drive.

Homosexuality and masturbation, referred to by Haredim as 'compulsiveness in sex', are not accepted by Haredim. Sex is not something that is to be enjoyed. (In the Gur sect within Haredi Judaism it is strictly prohibited to enjoy sex.)

Professor Bonne's justification for providing the antidepressants to Haredim is that this helps to avoid 'destructive conflicts that would make students depressed'. The medication 'enables them to preserve their place, image and dignity within the system, to continue to maintain proper family and social relations, and to find a match and raise a family'.

An initial question that arises is whether, from a religious point of view, medication is an acceptable, or the best means of complying with religious norms. One might think that, from a religious perspective, it is important to resist temptation through strength of mind. However, religious people already use 'tricks' to resist temptation, such as seeking distraction whenever 'inappropriate' sexual urges arise or having members of the opposite sex wear unrevealing dress. One further question then is whether the use of a pill is morally different from these non-biomedical tricks. It's difficult to see why it would be. Also, it may be that some people can *only* conform to religious norms by using medication; if one doesn't have the strength to resist temptation, maybe taking the pill is the next best option.

So should psychiatrists provide such 'treatments' if requested by the patient. The answer will depend on what role one ascribes to psychiatrists, and medical doctors in general. One view is that medical doctors should provide any medical services the patient demands, as long as these are legal and beneficial. Providing Haredim with antidepressants is legal. Is it beneficial for the 'patient'? This is controversial. The drugs might indirectly reduce depression by enabling the patient to think, feel, and act in accordance with the expected norms in his/her community. However, antidepressants have serious side effects and it is not clear that these are outweighed by the advantages of the drug (if there are any advantages at all). Also, perhaps having a good sex life is good for you, and the Haredim are mistaken to think otherwise.

But suppose there were safe drugs that reduced sexual desire. Should psychiatrists offer them to Haredim (or other religious groups with similar values) upon request? Since such treatment would be legal, and it is reasonable for an individual 'patient' to regard it as beneficial, it might seem that the psychiatrist should do so.

Perhaps one could say that helping people adhere to religious norms falls outside of the psychiatrist's sphere of duty and that, as a consequence, psychiatrists are not obliged to provide such 'treatment' even if requested by the patient. However, the aim of the drug could be described in several ways: to help maintain the Haredi community, or to increase people's well-being, for example, by increasing their authenticity (by helping them live in accordance with their deepest values), or by reducing anxiety and depression. The latter manifestly falls within the professional responsibility of psychiatrists.

Many psychiatrists will feel uncomfortable at the thought that they *should* provide such treatment. What, then, should they do?

Could they refuse to provide the treatment as a form of conscientious objection? Is it permissible for a psychiatrist to refuse providing a legal treatment that may be beneficial for the patient on the ground that she strongly objects to the values she would thereby promote? According to one philosopher in this area, 'values and conscience...should influence discussion on what kind of health system to deliver. But they should not influence the care an individual doctor offers to his or her patient. The door to "value-driven medicine" is a door to a Pandora's box of idiosyncratic, bigoted, discriminatory medicine.'[2] Following this reasoning, a psychiatrist would have no ground for conscientious objection. Yet my intuition is that individual psychiatrists should be able to refuse treatment because they do not want to be complicit in maintaining religious norms with which they profoundly disagree.

Conscientious objection is typically discussed in a context of objections to providing abortion services, contraceptives, terminal sedation to dying patients, or vaccines against sexually transmitted disease to young patients. In these cases, the question is typically whether doctors with conservative religious views are permitted to refuse treatments on the basis of those views. I share the intuition that it is problematic for them to do so. However, the question here is whether doctors with liberal moral views should be permitted to refuse treatments that they believe would make them complicit in religious views with which they disagree. Here my intuition is supportive of conscientious objection.

But this seems inconsistent and may be the result of a liberal bias on my part. Is the case of the Haredim really morally different from the case of, for example, prescribing contraceptive medicine?

It is difficult to see why conscientious objection should be more acceptable in the Haredim than the contraception case; if anything, the case seems weaker. Doctors who object to prescribing contraceptives often do so because they believe it would be gravely wrong; it would amount to murdering a person (the embryo), or at least exposing a person to a high risk of death. But surely no-one believes prescribing antidepressants to Haredim men is a comparably serious wrong. In this case, there is no third party whose life is at stake.

So the logic is clear, though, for me, uncomfortable. Rejecting conscientious objection in the contraceptive case commits us to rejecting it in the Haredim case too.

# Notes

1. Ettinger, Yair (6 April 2012). 'Rabbi's little helper', *Haaretz*. <http://www.haaretz.com/weekend/week-s-end/rabbi-s-little-helper-1.422985>
2. Savulescu, J. (2006). 'Conscientious objection in medicine', *British Medical Journal* 332/7536: 294–7, at p. 297; doi:10.1136/bmj.332.7536.294.

# RELIGION AND CHARITY

## 21

# CATHOLIC IDENTITY AND STRONG DISSENT—HOW COMPATIBLE?

Tony Coady

In previous writings I have made a number of radical criticisms of the Catholic Church's disciplinary practices, and of several of its prevailing 'official' teachings, such as those on artificial contraception, abortion, and much else in the area of sexual and reproductive ethics. Subsequently, several people put the question to me: 'Given your critical views of so much official church teaching, how can you still call yourself a Catholic?'

Those who raise this sort of question for 'liberal Catholics' seem to me captive to a certain view of adherence to the Catholic Church that I will call 'The Picture'. Their capture is understandable because The Picture had been assiduously cultivated by the church's leadership for generations. But recent turmoil in the Catholic Church has damaged The Picture severely as definitive of Catholic identity.

The Picture portrayed a proud monolith, firmly grounded in an array of crucial doctrines, disciplines, and ageless, immutable moral teachings that united all Catholics in a posture of certainty against heresy and the numerous errors of any given age. It not only served to fortify adherents, but attracted outsiders seeking certainty amidst what they saw as the gloom and confusion of modernity and its often strident, anti-religious outlook.

The first serious disfiguring of The Picture was made at Vatican Council II, which overturned in its wake such proud pillars as the Latin Mass, the Index of Prohibited Books, most mandated abstinence and fasting routines (such as meat-free Fridays), the almost total subservience of the laity to clerical authority in matters religious and sometimes secular, disdain for the non-Catholic world, denial of freedom of conscience, as well as much else previously bound up with Catholic identification. The central doctrine of 'no salvation outside the Church' was abandoned, or decisively diluted (depending on its interpretation), and conservatives rightly felt that much they held dear had mysteriously disappeared and much more was endangered. This feeling was accentuated by the widespread rejection in both word and deed amongst so many Catholics of Pope Paul VI's startling reaffirmation of the ban on artificial contraception in his 1968 encyclical *Humanae Vitae*. Later still, the revelations of extensive clerical sex abuse of children and the hierarchy's dismal attempts at concealment and deflection in the cause of preserving the status and authority of clerical leadership have further undermined that authority and the value of The Picture. This devaluing was most recently illustrated in 'Catholic Ireland's' 2015 referendum in favour of gay marriage in which the hierarchy's Catholic teaching was dramatically spurned.

Since the late 1960s, then, the church itself has been visibly divided into strongly opposed camps of 'conservatives' and 'liberals', though this division rather crudely conflates more subtle distinctions between members of the two groups. It might be better to speak of five groups— reactionaries, conservatives, moderates, liberals, and radicals—with many intersections between these groupings. So, among educated Catholics, and the ordinary faithful in the industrially advanced world, only a small group takes the ban on artificial contraception seriously. This small group also clings to much else that the other groups question, modify, or reject, and they hold fast to The Picture in spite of the evidence that it no longer represents reality.[1]

But the first thing to note is that, despite the undoubted power that The Picture has exerted for centuries, divergence and dissent from existing 'orthodoxy', moral and doctrinal, were always present, and in spite of repression and persecution often enough prevailed over time.

The philosophy and theology of St Thomas Aquinas was highly radical and controversial in his own life, and three years after his death it was condemned by the Bishop of Paris; centuries later it became, much to its detriment, the 'official' philosophy and central theology of the church. The German Dominican, Meister Eckhart, a key figure in the history of Christian mysticism, now widely respected in the Catholic Church, was in his own day accused of heresy and probably avoided execution by dying while Inquisition proceedings against him were underway. There are many other episodes in the chequered history of Catholic 'orthodoxy'. Nearer our time, the Australian nun, Mary MacKillop, was canonized Australia's first saint in 2010, though she had earlier been excommunicated by her Adelaide Archbishop for 'insubordination'. The radical shifts in official teaching about usury and about slavery are also important, though frequently ignored, aspects of change in Catholic orthodoxy, as is the dramatic modern shift in Catholic Biblical scholarship towards the mainstream, more historically oriented, Protestant paradigms.

The fact is that The Picture not only ignored history, but exerted a stifling hold on what it is to be a genuine Christian within the broad Catholic tradition. The issue of abortion is a good example of the disdain for history and for the possibility of fruitful dissent within the church. Up until roughly the seventeenth century, abortion was only condemned as basically a form of contraception and this condemnation was connected with an attitude to marital sex (gearing it exclusively to procreation) that the church gradually abandoned in the late twentieth century. The idea that the foetus was ensouled at the moment of conception was explicitly denied by Aquinas and many other Catholic authorities, so that the connection of early abortion with murder is a late and very dubious development.[2] The Picture encouraged a proliferation of defined or sharply mandated markers of Catholic identity in the form of a plethora of moral and religious propositions, disciplinary requirements, and rigid authoritarian structures, all of which are now in disarray. Moreover, the endeavour to fix a huge net of propositional rigidity around the idea of Catholic faith was a distortion of that strand in the Catholic tradition that honoured the place of a questing reason in religious life, exemplified by St Anselm's motto of faith seeking understanding ('fides quaerens intellectum'). Restricting such questing to an authorized clerical caste that then imposes edicts upon an unquestioning faithful does justice neither to faith nor reason. It issues in the ill-considered inflexibility of the prohibitions on married clergy and female ordination, the rigid prohibitions on divorce, the elevation into defined dogma of pious devotional beliefs such as Mary's Assumption into Heaven and her Immaculate Conception, and the intrinsically dubious concept of the Pope's defining himself into occasional infallibility.

Is there nothing that can be said to be crucial to Catholic identity? It all depends. In one sense, the vital contemporary question is not whether you identify as a Catholic, or Protestant, or Orthodox, but whether you are a Christian and so shape your life around the central Christian mysteries, such as the Incarnation, the Redemption, the Resurrection, and the urgent moral and spiritual messages of the Gospel.

This should give rise to a Christian ethic that is informed by such values as the central importance of neighbourly love (where neighbour is understood broadly as in Christ's parable of the Good Samaritan); the equality of all people as children of God and an associated concept of justice as more than a requirement of local institutions; the crucial importance of the poor and downtrodden as harbingers of God; the pre-eminent demands of peace; and the often mysterious significance of endured suffering. Much of this is perhaps more the province of ethos than codified ethic, but in conjunction with the efforts of natural reason it issues in distinctive, if contestable, injunctions to behaviour, including those involving the morality of homosexuality, divorce, abortion, and euthanasia, as well as broader issues such as capital punishment, racism, and immigration. These injunctions will sometimes overlap with non-Christian or non-religious moral conclusions, sometimes not. None of this should be surprising because we share a common reasoning and emotional nature, and, in addition, Christian (and Jewish) insights and values have shaped a great deal of Western and Eastern civilization, just as non-Christian thought has influenced Christian interpretation of its heritage.

As a Catholic, I try, in community with many others, to live in a complex, interpretive relation to those insights, values, and mysteries, and to the diverse strands that make up multi-coloured Catholic tradition. That tradition, already complex, is still in process of development—after all, the first two thousand years of Christianity may well prove to be its infancy, and the present turbulence within Catholicism a necessary stage of early healthy growth.

## Notes

1. I set aside here the interesting issue of the many Catholics, including distinguished intellectuals, who have abandoned the church since the

1960s partly in the belief that Catholic identity required commitment to The Picture.

2. See Dombrowski and Deltete (2007). *A Brief, Liberal Catholic Defense of Abortion* (Champaign, IL: University of Illinois Press). See also my review essay on the book (2003), 'Catholic identity and the abortion debate' in the US journal of the organization Catholics for Free Choice, *Conscience* XXIII/4.

# 22

# BANKING

*The ethical career choice*

William MacAskill

The High Pay Commission has just published a report denigrating the salaries of executives in the city.[1] This isn't unusual: it's common to see the astronomical pay of bankers and other city workers reviled in the media.

But there's a flip side to bankers' earnings, which often gets neglected. Wealth, of course, can be spent on champagne and yachts. But it can also be used to help people. In fact, I believe that if graduates spent their money wisely, they could usually do more good by following a lucrative career in banking—and donating a big chunk of their salary—than by pursuing a conventional 'ethical' career such as charity work. I call this approach 'earning-to-give'.

There are three reasons why earning-to-give is a promising path for altruistic graduates. First, the sheer amount one could potentially donate. Bankers will typically earn well over £6 million in their lifetime. By donating 50% of those earnings (bearing in mind that donations are not subject to income tax), a banker could pay for several charity workers—thereby doing several times as much good as if he or she had instead worked in the charity sector.

This can be expressed in stark terms. According to the latest estimates from GiveWell, it only costs about two thousand pounds to save a life in the developing world by distributing long-lasting insecticide-treated bednets.[2] By earning-to-give, donating 50% of one's income, a banker could in their career save over a thousand lives.

Secondly, different charities have varying degrees of effectiveness. According to the latest research from economists, some social programmes are hundreds of times more effective at improving lives with a given amount of resources than others. People who are earning-to-give can target their donations to only the most effective charities. In contrast, it's far more difficult to work only for the most effective charities, where there are only a few jobs available.

Finally, there are considerations of uncertainty. We should not be surprised if our current evidence about what the most important and effective causes are evolves over time. As external circumstances change and as some charities improve and others deteriorate, new opportunities to do good will arise. Someone who's earning-to-give can easily switch their donations in light of fresh information. In contrast, it's much more difficult to move jobs. It would invariably be easier to switch from funding anti-malarial nets to green technology than it would be to switch from working for a charity that fights malaria to working for a company that develops green technology.

Our choice of career is one of the most important decisions we make in life. But, currently, there's little advice on how best to choose a career that will have a big social impact. For that reason, I founded 80,000 Hours (the name referring to the number of hours that you will typically work in your life). The organization advises people on how they can best make a difference through their careers. A number of the graduates we advise have gone on to work in research, politics, entrepreneurship, and yes, in the non-profit sector. But, based on these arguments, hundreds of people around the world are now pursuing earning-to-give.[3] Some have donated hundreds of thousands of pounds after only a couple of years of work, significantly improving the lives of thousands of people.

We have a finite time on earth. But, if we're willing to think carefully about how to best use the 80,000 hours of our working life, I believe we can each have an extraordinary impact.[4]

## Notes

1. High Pay Commission (November 2011). 'Cheques with balances: why tackling high pay is in the national interest'. <http://highpaycentre.org/img/Cheques_with_Balances.pdf>
2. GiveWell (November 2011). 'Against Malaria Foundation: cost per life saved'. <http://www.givewell.org/international/top-charities/AMF#Costperlifesaved>

3. In a 2014 survey of the effective altruism community, 34.1% out of 813 respondents indicated that they were aiming to earn to give with their career, <http://effectivealtruismhub.com/sites/effectivealtruismhub.com/files/survey/2014/results-and-analysis.pdf> Examples of people in the 'effective altruism' community who've taken this path (though often not within finance) can be found at: <https://www.givingwhatwecan.org/about-us/members> Discussion of 80,0000 Hours' impact in particular can be found at: <https://80000hours.org/about/impact/>

4. For further reading, see <www.80000hours.org> and MacAskill, W. (2014). 'Replaceability, career choice, and making a difference', *Ethical Theory and Moral Practice* 17/2: 269–83.

# 23

# ON REBUILDING NOAH'S ARK AND DRINKING OLD BURGUNDY

Charles Foster

In North Kentucky, 40 miles from its Creation Museum (where you can see Eve riding on a triceratops and videos in which weeping girls blame their moral degeneracy on their failure to believe in the verbal inerrancy of Scripture), 'Answers in Genesis' is building a full-size replica of Noah's Ark. It's an expensive business. The total bill will be $29.5 million, of which $19,388,915 has been raised to date.[1] 'Partner with us in this amazing outreach by sponsoring a peg, plank or beam', pleads the website. A peg will cost you $100, a plank $1,000, and a beam $5,000. But if you buy a beam, you'll also get a model of the Ark personally signed by Ken Ham, the President of Answers in Genesis.

What's the point of all this? It's evangelism. 'Independent research has shown that millions will come to see it, and learn how it and the Flood were real events in history.' On that point at least, the research of Answers in Genesis is probably, and depressingly, correct.

I doubt very much whether there is any reader of this book who does not think that this is ridiculous. I expect that there are many who think that it is obscene. I am one of them. But why do I think that? It's true that it encourages people to believe that a myth is historically true. That's bad for them (since it's not good to believe palpable untruths), and bad for others (particularly since it helps to entrench the fundamentalists' corrosive, repercussive dogmatism, and because it scars the fair face of mythopoeia). But those offences, serious though they are, don't seem to justify the strength of the counter-reaction. So what is it?

The answer I came up with was that today about 40,000 children died of hunger, that the day's donations for pegs and planks would probably have saved them, that Christians are supposed to care about dying children, and that for the North Kentuckians to conclude that it was more important to convince people of the literal truth of the Noah story showed (1) that they had seriously calloused consciences, and (2) that they'd completely lost the plot of their own Christian story. I noted the darkly pleasing irony: Noah's Ark was supposedly used to save mankind, and yet the money spent on this Ark was money not spent on the real saving of real people. Ham's Ark, then, dooms rather than salvages.

I enjoyed my anger, since it seemed more righteous than most of my angry episodes. But then a friend pointed out that the money I spend on wine, one particular woman, and song, would keep quite a few from the grave. No doubt the good Young Earth Creationists rescue some too. Only some of their money goes on the Ark. The Ark is their frivolous, eccentric hobby, which gives a gruesome pleasure to mockers like me.

So is there any difference in principle between my entirely non-essential expenditure and their allocation of some of their money in trying to persuade people that the universe is 6,000 years old and that Noah's Ark landed on Ararat 4,500 years ago? Aren't they, in fact, rather better motivated than I am when I write cheques to Majestic Wines? OK, the Creationists are historically wrong; OK, they've failed to read properly their own creed's insistence on helping the poor. But their ignorance and confusion surely mitigate, not aggravate, their moral culpability in failing to spend their money more usefully. I, on the other hand, having had the thoughts expressed here, have no such excuse.

At the end of the film *Schindler's List* Oskar Schindler weeps as he calculates how many Jewish lives he could have bought had he sold his gold pin or his car. I have had that scene on continuous loop, trying to escape from the terrifying logic of his arithmetic. I can see no escape. Certainly Ken Ham's absurdities can't help me.

Will the burgundy stop flowing? I doubt it. I'm a hypocrite.

But it does mean that I've bookmarked this site <http://www.givingwhatwecan.org/>

# Note

1. As of May 2015. See <https://arkencounter.com/>

## 24

# SHOULD CONSERVATIVE CHRISTIANS BE ALLOWED TO FOSTER CHILDREN?

Simon Rippon

Eunice and Owen Johns are conservative Christians who believe that sexual relations other than those within marriage between one man and one woman are morally wrong. They also want to be foster parents, caring for children placed with them on a short-term basis by the local authority. Should they be allowed to care for other people's children?

The Johns's local authority rejected their application to be foster carers. Their appeal went up to England's High Court, which ruled against the Johns in 2011.[1] I won't say whether the court was right or wrong about English law. But what *ought* the law to say about cases like this? I believe that, with one proviso, people like Eunice and Owen Johns should be allowed to foster, because anything else would be *illiberal*.

What were the Johns's attitudes about homosexuality? According to the court's opinion, the Johns had previously expressed an inability to support 'a young person who was confused about their sexuality'. They believed that homosexuality is 'against God's laws and morals'. Owen Johns said that if a young person in his care thinks he or she might be gay, he would 'gently turn them around'. Eunice Johns said that she once visited San Francisco, a city famous for its large gay population, and that she felt uncomfortable there and disliked it.

The Johns's attitudes to homosexuality are, I believe, ignorant and wrong. Even if you want to derive your ethical guidance from Jesus's teachings, the fact that Jesus is never recorded mentioning homosexuality should give you pause. And if you believe homosexuality is wrong because the Apostle Paul said so, then you ought to take Paul's views about women and gender-specific headwear just as seriously:

> 3 … Christ is the head of every man, and the man is the head of a woman … 4 Every man who has something on his head while praying or prophesying disgraces his head. 5 But every woman who has her head uncovered while praying or prophesying disgraces her head … 7 For a man ought not to have his head covered, since he is the image and glory of God; but the woman is the glory of man. 8 For man does not originate from woman, but woman from man; 9 for indeed man was not created for the woman's sake, but woman for the man's sake.  (1 Corinthians 11:3–9)[2]

But I digress.

What the court had to decide in the Johns's case was how to balance competing values. On the one hand, the state aims to be neutral between religions, tolerant of religious diversity, and respectful of religious beliefs. On the other hand, there is concern about the potential impact on the welfare of children. As the Justices wrote in the court's opinion, the fact that a believer is acting on a conscientious religious belief cannot immunize the action from an otherwise valid legal claim. Some cultural and religious practices—such as female genital mutilation—may be treated by the law as beyond the pale, even if they are rooted in cultural or religious tradition. The Justices highlighted a possible tension between the Johns's Christian beliefs and the welfare of children in their care: 'If children, whether they are known to be homosexuals or not, are placed with carers who … evince an antipathy, objection to or disapproval of, homosexuality and same-sex relationships, there may well be a conflict with the local authority's duty to "safeguard and promote" the "welfare" of looked-after children.' Consequently, the court found that local authorities are entitled to consider prospective foster carers' beliefs when these may affect their treatment of a child in care.

How could I disagree with such an eminently reasonable approach? Well, I start by noting that just like their local authority, the Johns *also* consider themselves to be concerned with the welfare of children. They sincerely believe that failing to 'gently turn around' a young person who thinks they might be homosexual would be akin to failing to direct the child away from an addiction to heroin, or a career in shoplifting, or some other waste of life and talent.

'But the Johns are *mistaken!*' you may reply. 'A young person's welfare consists in part in *embracing* his or her developing sexual identity, and in his or her ability to *celebrate* diversity of sexual orientation. It is *wrong* to think that having a developing homosexual interest, for a young adult, is in any way like having a developing interest in hard drugs or crime.'

I would agree. But the issue here is not my personal opinion or yours; it is whether the state should make a judgement about this issue. It should not. To see why, consider what might happen if conservative Christians like Eunice and Owen Johns were a majority of the English population, and determined guidelines for carers with their votes. Suppose also that they based their judgement on what they thought was in the interests of the comprehensive welfare of children. Wouldn't they decide that those potential carers who would ignore, or even approve of and encourage, homosexual tendencies or behaviour would be *at best* woefully negligent in their care? This imagined majority would surely insist that *only* those who are willing to treat homosexuality as morally unacceptable are qualified to care for children.

Our imagined conservative Christian majority may be mistaken in their judgements about what is in a child's welfare. But that is not the point. In our society there is deep disagreement about many moral issues. This means that we cannot hope to reach consensus on comprehensive views about what is in every child's best interests. If we are to avoid the tyranny of a majority that seeks to impose its comprehensive value system on others, we must agree to limit the interference of government with our privately held moral values.

According to the philosopher John Rawls, government should be organized so that it enables individuals, as far as possible, to form and pursue their own comprehensive conceptions of the good, and government ought generally to maintain neutrality between different conceptions of the good.[3] This is the doctrine of political liberalism. Reasonable people, Rawls says, will form an overlapping consensus around this liberal principle; agreeing that each may pursue what he regards as good, so long as his pursuit does not infringe on the ability of others to do the same. In the liberal state, government is not concerned with promoting any particular conception of the good, but only with promoting liberal citizenship: the ability of each to form and pursue his own preferred conception of the good.

The Rawlsian politically liberal state would still regulate foster carers and would certainly deny some people permission to look after the children of others. But it would not do so on the grounds of any particular comprehensive conception of the welfare of children. It would concern itself only with ensuring that children were enabled to grow up to be well-functioning, liberal citizens, capable of making their own autonomous choices about how to live.

Here we come to the liberal provisos about people like Eunice and Owen Johns. They need not approve of homosexual behaviour to be carers in the liberal state; indeed they would be entitled to express their strong religious opinions. But they must be willing to nurture any child in their care even while they may overtly disapprove of that child's sexual orientation, or that of others, and they must be willing to provide the child with the resources and information needed to let the child decide, as he or she grew older, how best to live. The liberal state would not allow carers to inculcate views that fundamentally conflict with political liberalism, nor generally to engage in indoctrination. But any carers willing to meet these provisos could qualify, whatever their personal moral and religious beliefs.

By refusing to endorse any particular comprehensive conception of the welfare of children, the liberal state would be even-handed and non-judgemental in its demands: pro-homosexual dogmatists would be just as unwelcome to apply to be carers as homophobic dogmatists. This is why the liberal state represents an attractive compromise between conflicting comprehensive conceptions of the good.

It is, then, the fairest form of government we can reasonably hope for.

# Notes

1. <http://www.bailii.org/ew/cases/EWHC/Admin/2011/375.html>
2. <http://biblehub.com/nasb/1_corinthians/11.htm>
3. Rawls, J. (1993). *Political Liberalism* (New York: Columbia University Press).

# SEX, SEX-EQUALITY, AND SEXUALITY

# 25

# CAN YOU BE GAY BY CHOICE?

Brian D. Earp

Can you be gay by choice? Most campaigners for gay rights would say no. But in January 2012, former *Sex and the City* star Cynthia Nixon—who identifies as gay—said that she *chose* her sexual orientation from among alternatives. In an interview, she put it like this:

> I gave a speech recently, an empowerment speech to a gay audience, and it included the line 'I've been straight and I've been gay, and gay is better.' And they tried to get me to change it, because they said it implies that homosexuality can be a choice. And for me, it is a choice. I understand that for many people it's not, but for me it's a choice, and you don't get to define my gayness for me.

She went on to say: 'A certain section of our community is very concerned that it not be seen as a choice, because if it's a choice, then we could opt out. [But] why can't it be a choice? Why is that any less legitimate? It seems we're just ceding this point to bigots who are demanding it.'[1]

What were some members of the gay community worried about? The concern was this: if people can't choose who they're sexually attracted to, then it seems unfair to discriminate against them on account of their sexual orientation. For that would be like discriminating against someone because of their race or sex, which are equally un-chosen (because both are determined at birth). But if too many members of the public were to take Nixon's statements seriously, it would have the effect of undermining the 'born this way' movement for gay rights, which is largely premised on the idea that people can't choose their sexual orientations.

# The question of identity

Now it's my turn to weigh in. I think that Cynthia Nixon is a lot closer to correct on this issue than her detractors. 'Being gay'—as opposed to 'feeling uncontrollably and exclusively attracted to same-sex individuals'—is a question of identity, and one's identity is in many respects up to oneself. That is, it is a question of how one chooses to self-identify. If you think you're gay, then you're gay.

Now, if you find yourself overwhelmingly attracted to members of the opposite sex, and not at all to members of the same sex (of course these are over-simplifications—sex is not a simple binary), you would be a bad citizen of your language community to go on and apply the label 'gay' to yourself. You'd be bound to cause some confusion. We *don't*, as a rule, get to make up our own new personal meanings for words and expect others to play along.

But if you're capable of feeling attraction to members of more than one sex, as many people are, and if you orient your romantic and sexual behaviour around the same-sex side of the continuum, then go ahead and consider yourself gay. Who you 'are' is not a metaphysical fact. Instead, it's a self-constructed tag, used for the sake of convenience to dumb down the complexity of interpersonal judgements and communication. A tag is a placeholder for a longer conversation. 'Gay' is tag.

The question of who a person is *chiefly sexually attracted to*, across time and circumstance, is less up for debate, and is largely a *different* question. And it is one that can be answered—so far as we know—by appeals to both nature and nurture.[2] Genes play a role. Early experiences (like exposure to certain hormones in the womb) play a role. People's attitudes toward their own sexual feelings play a role, and so on. For many people, these various factors conspire to push the weight of attraction very heavily to one side of the sex-based physical appearance scale or the other.

For others it's more ambiguous. In fact, chopping up human sexuality into a few nifty labels—'gay', 'straight', and 'bisexual'—is the source of much confusion here. Sexual attraction is complex, and the labels are shorthand. If you want to *really* know about a person's sexual orientation, you should be prepared to sit and chat with them for a while.

## Getting back to choice

So where does this leave us? If what I've said so far is correct, then, for some people, there certainly *is* room for choice with respect to their 'gayness', and Cynthia Nixon is one such individual. But still, it might be asked, isn't there an important difference between making a decision about how to self-identify—or even how to *act* on the basis of one's innermost sexual desires—and actually changing the desires themselves? And if *those* (the desires) are largely determined by biological factors outside of a person's control, then wouldn't it still be unfair to discriminate against people with predominately same-sex sexual attractions?

Yes, that's right. Fair enough. But there's an even deeper problem to resolve. For if sexual orientation is largely 'written into' the brain by the forces of neurochemistry—as science seems to suggest, and as the 'born this way' gay rights movement has been at pains to make public knowledge—then actually *changing* that neurochemistry (in the right kind of way) would allow people to change their sexual orientation after all.

Such 'hi-tech' conversion therapy is not currently available.[3] But one day, it very well might be. So, what should we be prepared to conclude? That if people *can* eventually change their sexual orientations, it would be OK to discriminate against those who choose to stick with their same-sex attraction?

## Conclusion

This takes us back to Cynthia Nixon and her 'bigots'—those people who want to deny equal rights to same-sex couples. To draw such a conclusion, she suggested, would be to allow the (homophobic) religious right to 'define the terms of the debate'. And she's right: the debate shouldn't hinge on the question of choice. To see why this is the case, consider the following perspective of Dan Savage, the well-known social commentator.

'Religious conservatives go on TV,' he writes, 'and knock on doors, [and] distribute pamphlets, [and] proselytize, and evangelize all over the country in an effort to get people to do what? To change their religions. To choose a different faith.' In other words:

faith—religious belief—is not an immutable characteristic. You can change your faith. And yet religious belief is covered by civil rights laws and anti-discrimination statutes . . . The only time you hear that a trait has to be immutable in order to qualify for civil rights protections is when [conservatives] talk about [being] gay.[4]

The moral goal is clear. Gay people—including those whose feelings of attraction are largely outside of their control, as well as those who have some elbow room in terms of their feelings or notions of identity—deserve to be treated with respect. And romantic gay relationships are no less worthy of social and legal support than so-called straight relationships. So, as long as the state is involved in regulating marriage (and it isn't clear that it should be), it should not be permitted to deny its citizens equal treatment before the law, whatever their sexual orientation.[5]

# Notes

1. Witchell, A. (19 January 2012). 'Life after "sex"', *New York Times*. <http://www.nytimes.com/2012/01/22/magazine/cynthia-nixon-wit.html?_r=0>
2. Vierra, A. and Earp, B. D. (21 April 2015). 'Born this way? How high-tech conversion therapy could undermine gay rights', *The Conversation*. <https://theconversation.com/born-this-way-how-high-tech-conversion-therapy-could-undermine-gay-rights-40121>
3. Earp, B. D., Sandberg, A., and Savulescu, J. (2014). 'Brave new love: the threat of high-tech conversion therapy and the bio-oppression of sexual minorities', *AJOB Neuroscience* 5/1: 4–12.
4. Savage, D. (4 March 2015). 'Ben Carson: being gay is a choice and prison proves it', *The Stranger*. <http://www.thestranger.com/blogs/slog/2015/03/04/21827375/republican-idiot-being-gay-is-a-choice-and-prison-proves-it>
5. See Vierra and Earp, note 2.

# 26

# PROSTITUTION AND DISABILITY

Brian D. Earp

Is prostitution harmful? If it is harmful, should it be illegal to buy (or sell) sexual services? And, if so, should there ever be exceptions?

What about for people with certain disabilities, say, who might find it difficult or even impossible to find a sexual partner if they were barred from exchanging money for sex? Do people have a 'right' to sexual fulfillment?[1]

In a fascinating recent essay in the *Journal of Medical Ethics*, the philosopher Frej Klem Thomsen explores[2] these and other controversial questions. His focus is on the issue of *exceptions*—specifically for those with disabilities. According to Thomsen, a person is 'relevantly disabled' (for the sake of this discussion) if and only if:

(1) she has sexual needs, and desires to exercise her sexuality, and
(2) she has an anomalous physical or mental condition that, given her social circumstances, sufficiently limits her possibilities of exercising her sexuality, including fulfilling her sexual needs.[3]

There is a lot to say here. First, in order to sort out the merits of making an *exception* to a general ban on prostitution (for people with disabilities or for anyone else), we would normally want to start by deciding what to think about the advisability of such a ban in the first place. For, if we didn't think it was a good idea to begin with, then we could skip all the talk about making an exception, and just argue against an overall ban.

Now, as it happens, some philosophers,[4] social scientists,[5] and others who have studied this issue in detail, have argued that prohibiting prostitution is in fact a bad idea, all things considered. In their view, such a policy actually *increases* the level of harm to prostitutes (or sex workers), because—among other issues—it forces the practice underground. Other authors, however, strongly disagree with this conclusion.[6] As they see it, prohibiting prostitution does not in fact increase the level of harm to prostitutes, whereas legalizing prostitution does.

The debate goes on and on.[7] Since there is no clear consensus on the issue, we are going to just assume for the sake of argument—as Thomsen does in his essay—that paying for sexual services should be illegal as a matter of course. Granting this assumption, the question becomes: is there a compelling case to be made for an *exception* to this rule for people with disabilities?

## The case for an exception

Thomsen points to two facts that lay the groundwork for his position:

(1) Many or most persons have a sexuality that generates strong needs for sexual relations.

(2) Some disabled persons are partially or entirely incapable of satisfying this need except through the purchase of sexual services from a prostitute.[8]

Let me give you an example of what he means. Quoting from another source,[9] he cites the case of a man who couldn't walk and was taken to a prostitute (or sex worker) by his carer. 'You had to lift him out of the wheelchair and into the Jacuzzi and he was stiff because he didn't move his arms or legs. He couldn't move, [he] could get an erection but that was about it.'[10]

What should we say about a case like this?

The first thing to point out is that the man's disability didn't make it so that he *physically couldn't have sex* (if that were the case, hiring a prostitute would not help his situation); instead, the issue was more that he *couldn't (otherwise) find a willing sexual partner*, for whatever reason.

Now, it seems reasonable to conclude that—in this particular instance—the 'reason' had something to do with his physical disability. In other words, it seems likely that (all else being equal) relatively few people would desire, as their first choice, to form a sexual relationship with someone who could not 'move his arms or legs' (although I imagine that there are many exceptions).

But that is a specific case and it glosses over a more general point. And that is that all sorts of people find it difficult to find a willing sexual partner—or enough willing sexual partners—to 'satisfy their sexual needs', for a whole range of reasons that have nothing to do with physical disability of the 'obvious' kind exemplified by this man. Such people may simply be perceived as unattractive, based on the prevailing aesthetic norms of their community. Or they may be shy, or have intense anxiety in social situations. Alternatively, they may have none of these (or other similar) problems, but rather an insatiable sexual appetite. Are all of these people 'disabled' on Thomsen's account?

## Defining disability

Thomsen has a dilemma. On the one hand, he could define 'disability' in a very narrow sense that captures only the 'obvious' cases that everyone would recognize—perhaps typified by the man in the example. But this would result in an extremely unreliable and almost absurdly arbitrary proxy for the 'real' underlying issue at stake, which is the difficulty that some people have in finding a willing sexual partner(s) sufficient to meet their sexual needs, without having recourse to payment.

After all, many people with physical and/or mental disabilities have perfectly satisfying sexual relationships; and many people without such disabilities have unsatisfying—or no—sexual relationships (for any number of unrelated reasons). Thus there is no direct or necessary connection between 'having a disability' of some kind and being perceived as sexually undesirable.

On the other hand, Thomsen could define 'disability' in a very broad sense—which is what he does in fact choose to do. But this carries its own set of problems. For one thing, it picks out a vague and amorphous group of people who (to quote from Thomsen's definition) have 'an anomalous physical or mental condition that, given [their] social circumstances, sufficiently limits [their] possibilities of exercising [their] sexuality, including fulfilling [their] sexual needs'.[11]

But that could include just about anyone! For one thing, there is the nearly boundless room for interpretation surrounding most of the key terms in Thomsen's definition: 'anomalous', 'physical', 'mental', 'condition', 'sufficiently', and 'fulfill' (just to start). For example, what is 'anomalous'? Statistically rare? How rare? As measured along what dimension? Also, why should the condition have to be 'anomalous' in any event? Isn't it the (lack of) functional outcome that is the morally relevant concern?

Or think about the word 'condition'—meaning what? Is shyness (to repeat that example) a 'mental condition' that counts as a disability? And what about 'sufficiently'? How shall we determine the cut-off? In other words, just how 'hard' does it have to be to find a willing sexual partner before one is allowed to register oneself as 'sexually disabled', say, and pick up her 'prostitution exemption' card? And finally—'fulfill'. Wouldn't, say, most married couples report that their sexual needs were not 'fulfilled' in some relevant way? Indeed, one survey puts the figure at 57%.[12]

## Conclusion

So this doesn't seem to be the way to go. Either the definition of disability is so narrow as to be unjustifiably arbitrary as a proxy for the real underlying moral issue, or it's so broad as to include almost anyone. An alternative approach, then, would be to argue against a general prohibition and in favour of letting mature individuals decide for themselves (1) what kind of consensual sex they wish to engage in and (2) in exchange for what.[13]

## Notes

1. For the purposes of this chapter, we are going to assume that all such transactions are truly consensual: freely entered into by both (or all) relevant parties. Now, some people think that this can never really happen. As they see it, no one would ever accept money in exchange for sex unless they were 'forced' to do so by their circumstances. According to this view, all such transactions are inherently coercive. However, other people disagree with this kind of analysis, including many self-identified sex workers and at least some feminist moral philosophers. For further discussion, see Weinberg, J., de Marneffe, P., Demetriou, D., Earp, B.D., Fuller, L., Gauthier, J., Hay, C., Marino, P., Pettit, P., and Whisnant, R. (13 August 2015). 'Philosophers on prostitution's decriminalization', *Daily Nous*. <https://www.academia.edu/14907902/Philosophers_on_prostitutions_decriminalization>

2. Thomsen, F. K. (2015). 'Prostitution, disability and prohibition', *Journal of Medical Ethics* 41/6: 451–9.

3. Thomsen, p. 455.
4. E.g., Moen, O. M. (2014). 'Is prostitution harmful?', *Journal of Medical Ethics* 40/2: 73–81; Moen, O. M. (2014). 'Prostitution and harm: a reply to Anderson and McDougall', *Journal of Medical Ethics* 40/2: 84–5.
5. E.g., Wolffers, I. and van Beelen, N. (2003). 'Public health and the human rights of sex workers', *Lancet* 361/9373: 1981.
6. E.g., Farley, M. (2004). '"Bad for the body, bad for the heart": prostitution harms women even if legalized or decriminalized', *Violence Against Women* 10/10: 1087–125. But see Weitzer, R. (2005). 'Flawed theory and method in studies of prostitution', *Violence Against Women* 11/7: 934–49.
7. Weinberg et al.
8. Thomsen, p. 455.
9. Sanders, T. (2007). 'The politics of sexual citizenship: commercial sex and disability', *Disability & Society* 22/5: 439–55.
10. Thomsen, p. 455.
11. Thomsen, p. 455.
12. National Survey of Marital Strengths. <https://www.prepare-enrich.com/pe_main_site_content/pdf/research/national_survey.pdf>
13. This chapter is adapted from: Earp, B. D. (2015). 'Prostitution, harm, and disability: should only people with disabilities be allowed to pay for sex?' *Journal of Medical Ethics,* e-letter. <https://www.academia.edu/13252176/Prostitution_harm_and_disability_Should_only_people_with_disabilities_be_allowed_to_pay_for_sex>

# 27

# ARTIFICIAL WOMBS AND
# A VISIT TO BIRLAND

## Chris Gyngell

In 2012 scientists successfully used an artificial uterus to bring shark embryos to term.[1] Once 'birthed' the shark pups showed no detrimental effects as a result of having gone through development in an artificial setting.

Research such as this ignites interest in the possibility of creating artificial wombs for the purpose of human reproduction. After all, artificial hearts, kidneys, and lungs are all available and becoming increasingly sophisticated. It is surely only a matter of time before artificial wombs, capable of growing and developing a foetus outside the human body, are technologically feasible.

This raises a simple question: should we promote research aimed at shifting the location of foetal development to outside the human body? To answer this, let's take a trip to another world—Birland.

\* \* \*

In Birland a species exists that is identical to humans in nearly every way—they are called the Birmans. The major difference between humans and Birmans is evolutionary history. Rather than evolving from mammals, Birmans evolved from birds. As a result, nearly all of the development and growth of Birman foetuses occurs outside their bodies in eggs. However, this could soon change. Birman scientists believe they are on the verge of developing 'internal wombs' which would allow Birman foetuses to develop inside the body of a parent. As a result of this development, a group of Birman ethicists and policy-makers discuss the possible costs and benefits of changing the location of foetal development to inside the body.

The first cost they identify is equality. Currently both Birman sexes have an equal role in the development of foetuses. This would be fundamentally changed if foetal development occurred inside the body. This is because, for physiological reasons, internal pregnancies would only be viable in females. All of the costs and benefits associated with nurturing a foetus inside the body would, therefore, be imposed on just one sex.

The second worry is health and safety. An individual's body would be changed significantly to accommodate a developing foetus. Abdominal muscles would be separated, skin would be stretched, and extra strain would be placed on blood vessels. This would increase the risk of a range of mild health conditions and could cause long-term damage to the muscles and skin. More significantly, the birthing of the baby once it is fully developed would likely be difficult for some Birman women. The only way the fully developed foetus could leave the body without surgery is through the pelvis. However, as a result of evolutionary adaptations for bipedalism, the Birman pelvis is relatively small and the heads of Birman infants are relatively large. Therefore, birth would be risky for some women and result in ongoing complications such as incontinence and internal tissue tearing. In fact scientists estimate that in approximately 15% of cases the baby would not be able to leave the body naturally and surgery would be required. This surgery would carry with it a small risk of paralysis and death for the mother.

The third concern identified by the Birmans involves freedom. Given foetuses are highly sensitive to disturbances, growing one inside someone's body would restrict that individual's ability to participate in a range of activities. For instance, a pregnant woman would not be able to engage in very strenuous exercise, play certain sports, drink much caffeine or alcohol, or take certain medications—without endangering the foetus. Hormone changes at the beginning of pregnancy would sometimes result in nausea, and the extra energy requirements towards the end of pregnancy would lead to lethargy. The gestation period would be very long—9 months—and during this entire period individuals would face considerable constraints on their liberty.

The final cost of internal pregnancies is the safety of the foetus. Some individuals would be unlikely to stop themselves from consuming drugs and alcohol while the foetus is developing, and this could result in permanent damage. In fact, it is estimated that if the intervention was widespread, individuals drinking alcohol while pregnant would become one of the leading causes of developmental problems in Birman children. The birth is also expected to be risky for Birman infants. Nerve damage, infections, and dystocia are all possible complications associated with birth from an internal pregnancy.

When considering the possible benefits of moving foetal development to inside the body, one expert suggests that it would deepen the bond between mother and child. But other Birman policy-makers are unconvinced. They point out that there is little empirical evidence to back up this claim, and argue that parents who are not biologically related to their children are perfectly able to form strong bonds with them.

Given the potential risks involved, Birman ethicists decide that they have good reasons to keep developing their foetuses in external eggs. For creatures with their characteristics, internal pregnancies would be far too costly for both mother and child.

*　*　*

This hypothetical scenario has direct relevance to debates on the ethics of human artificial wombs. The only reason that human foetuses develop inside the body of their mothers is evolutionary history—we have evolved from a long line of species who nurtured their young internally. While this made sense for the first placental mammals, humans today are very different to these ancestors. We walk on two legs, have large brains, and don't need to worry about predators eating eggs containing our young. The same reasons that make it irrational for Birmans to use internal wombs suggest humans should embrace the possibility of external wombs.

# Note

1. Otway, N. and Ellis, M. (2012). 'Construction and test of an artificial uterus for ex situ development of shark embryos', *Zoo Biology* 31: 197–205.

# 28

# IS UNWANTED PREGNANCY
# A MEDICAL DISORDER?

Rebecca Roache

Abortion has long been a contested ethical issue, but we could reduce the suffering caused by abortion without taking a stand on whether or not it is ethical. Both sides can concede that abortion causes suffering, and that we can best reduce this by reducing unwanted pregnancies. I believe that current efforts to reduce unwanted pregnancies are not good enough, and that we could do better by viewing unwanted pregnancy as a medical disorder.

That abortion causes suffering to foetuses is a major claim in the pro-life argument, and unwanted pregnancy and abortion are traumatic for women, too. But banning abortion also results in suffering: almost half of the estimated 44 million abortions that occur worldwide each year are unsafe (i.e. carried out by unskilled individuals, using hazardous equipment, or in unsanitary facilities).[1] Countries where abortion is banned have far higher rates of unsafe abortion.[2]

Since both permitting and banning abortion result in significant suffering, it is concerning how ineffective existing efforts are to reduce demand for abortions. While the UK runs sex-education programmes and provides free contraception, in 2011 there were nearly one hundred and ninety thousand UK abortions. The UK has the highest teenage birth and abortion rates in Western Europe, and those seeking abortions report being unaware of their contraceptive choices, misunderstanding how to use contraception, or not using it at all.[3] How can we do better?

I suggest that we should view unwanted pregnancy as a medical disorder and aggressively promote contraception the way we promote vaccination. Unwanted pregnancy, after all, can be as devastating as some serious diseases. A woman with an unwanted pregnancy faces a choice between a (legal and safe, if she's lucky) medical procedure to end the pregnancy, or huge life changes for which she may be emotionally and financially unprepared.

Does it matter that unwanted pregnancy does not involve biological malfunctioning? No: many disorders and disabilities do not involve the body malfunctioning in any specific way. Many mental disorders, which lack clear tissue or molecular pathologies, take this form. And some campaigners argue that disabilities like deafness are not biological malfunctions but social constructs.

Currently, unwanted pregnancy is viewed as a social problem. As such, it tends to be addressed through education and public awareness campaigns. Taking seriously the idea that unwanted pregnancy is a disorder may encourage more effective prevention methods, like medical ones. Parents could be encouraged to obtain contraception for their (fertile) children the way they are encouraged to have their children vaccinated. By 'encouraged', I do not mean 'given leaflets'. I mean that, when children reach adolescence, their parents should be asked to bring them to a clinic to be prescribed contraceptives—ideally implants, injections, or other methods whose effectiveness does not depend on the patient's cooperation. As with routine childhood vaccination programmes, participation should not be compulsory, but social pressure should be applied to ensure a high level of uptake.

There are likely to be objections to the idea that we should promote contraception the way we promote vaccination. I will try to anticipate some of them.

*Freedom*: Would the scheme I have outlined infringe on young people's freedom to make their own contraceptive choices, and on parents' freedom to choose how to raise their children? Not really. Since this scheme would not be coercive, it would not infringe on freedom any more than promoting vaccination does. And since ineffective use of contraception results in unwanted pregnancy, which curtails freedom by limiting choices, the current failure to promote contraception is, surely, a greater infringement on freedom.

*Encouraging promiscuity*: We sometimes hear that promoting contraception to young people might encourage them to have sex. I can think of two main reasons—beside unwanted pregnancy—why people might object to this. First, there are sexually transmitted diseases (STDs). The types of contraception I have advocated promoting do not protect against STDs and this might deter young people from using barrier methods that *do* protect against STDs. However, I have described a system in which young people are routinely summoned to a clinic to receive contraception. They can be educated about barrier methods while they are there. It would be surprising if this system would *increase* irresponsible sexual behaviour. Second, some might worry that young people having more sex is a bad thing regardless of the consequences. This resembles the 1960s anxiety, when the contraceptive pill became available, that women would become more promiscuous and that relationships between men and women would change. This is exactly what did happen: women now have children later in life and enjoy sexual relationships that do not result in children. This might have horrified social commentators in the 1960s, but society has changed; few now regard these developments as negative. This should caution us against placing too much weight on non-consequentialist worries about sexual promiscuity among young people today.

*Sexism*: Implanted and injectable contraceptives are not available for men, so, in practice, my system would only target women. It would subject women but not men to medical treatment to prevent a problem caused by both men and women, and it might also encourage the view that contraception is women's responsibility. Is this sexist? It would be better if the programme targeted men and women equally, as it may do when male hormonal contraceptives become available. Even so, what I have proposed aims to prevent unwanted pregnancies, which affect women more than men. It is unlikely that any negative consequences for women of these measures would outweigh the current negative effects of dealing with hundreds of thousands of unwanted pregnancies in the UK alone.

Whilst the long-vexed abortion debate is motivated by concerns about the welfare, rights, and interests of foetuses and their mothers, all sides of the debate can agree that it would be better for both women and foetuses if fewer abortions were required. Working harder to prevent unwanted pregnancies is the obvious way of achieving this, and I have outlined a way in which this could happen cost-effectively and using current medical technology.

# Notes

1. <http://www.fpa.org.uk/factsheets/teenage-pregnancy>
2. Shah, I., et al. (2009). 'Unsafe abortion: global and regional incidence, trends, consequences, and challenges', *Journal of Obstetrics and Gynaecology Canada* 31/12: 1149–58.
3. <https://www.gov.uk/government/uploads/system/uploads/attachment_data/file/213386/Commentary1.pdf>

## 29

# IS HALF AN ABORTION
# WORSE THAN A
# WHOLE ONE?

Simon Rippon

The *New York Times Magazine* has run an article by Ruth Padawer profiling women who chose to undergo a procedure that many readers found ethically disturbing—an elective 'reduction' of their twin pregnancies to a singleton.[1]

The article recounted the emotions and ethical issues grappled with by the women, their partners, and their doctors. The procedure, usually performed around the end of the first trimester, involves the doctor selecting under ultrasound scan a healthy foetus whose chest is lethally injected. It dies and shrivels in the womb, whilst its twin is carried to term. In the cases in question, the reduction is not performed for medical reasons, but because the woman has chosen for social reasons to carry only one child to term. Although reductions arose historically as a procedure that was medically indicated—reducing risky quint, quad, or triplet pregnancies to twins that had a much better chance of survival—most practitioners do not consider reduction below twins to have a medical justification. Some doctors nevertheless perform twin reductions willingly. As Dr Richard Berkowitz explained: 'In a society where women can terminate a single pregnancy for any reason— financial, social, emotional—if we have a way to reduce a twin pregnancy with very little risk, isn't it legitimate to offer that service to women with twins who want to reduce to a singleton?' Dr Berkowitz's question is a good one, as is the main question that Padawer raises: 'What is it about terminating half a twin pregnancy that seems more controversial than reducing triplets to twins or aborting a single foetus? After all, the math's the same either way: one fewer fetus.'

Padawer's article raised moral doubts and questions among pro-choicers and feminists, including authors on the blog *Jezebel* and *Slate* magazine.[2,3] One conservative op-ed mocked the 'anguished liberals' under the headline 'The Failure of Liberal Bioethics'.[4] So what *is* it that makes terminating half a twin pregnancy seem more controversial than aborting a single foetus? Does our almost universal queasiness about this procedure show a fundamental inconsistency in pro-choice thinking, or is there a consistent pro-choice position that pays sufficient respect both to a woman's right to choose, and to our uneasy intuitive reactions to twin reduction?

In reflecting on these questions, it is worth considering what kind of specific reasons parents might have for pursuing twin reduction. 'Jenny', a mother of school age children who was wealthy enough to have spent thousands of dollars on six years of fertility treatment before conceiving again at the age of 45, was quoted in Padawer's article:

> Things would have been different if we were 15 years younger or if we hadn't had children already or if we were more financially secure...If I had conceived these twins naturally, I wouldn't have reduced this pregnancy, because you feel like if there's a natural order, then you don't want to disturb it. But we created this child in such an artificial manner—in a test tube...and somehow, making a decision about how many to carry seemed to be just another choice. The pregnancy was all so consumerish to begin with, and this became yet another thing we could control.

Padawer adds that,

> Jenny's decision to reduce twins to a single fetus was never really in doubt. The idea of managing two infants at this point in her life terrified her...She felt that twins would soak up everything she had to give, leaving nothing for her older children. Even the twins would be robbed, because, at best, she could give each one only half of her attention and, she feared, only half of her love. Jenny desperately wanted another child, but not at the risk of becoming a second-rate parent.

There is plenty to dispute about Jenny's characterization of her reasons for seeking twin reduction. No doubt none is in a stronger position to dispute her claims than the many successful mothers of multiples who would bristle at the suggestion that there has been anything 'second-rate' about their parenting because of their necessarily divided attention. Jenny also drew an odd connection between the rightness of her decision to pursue reduction and the fact that her pregnancy was not 'natural'. Together with her rigid focus on providing not less than a certain amount of financial and emotional resources for each of her children, this suggests that she aimed at a kind of 'designer' family. But it is impossible to exert the degree of control over one's family that Jenny seems to aspire to. Jenny might well be advised to revise her attitudes and learn to live with less control rather than trying to exert more, on the grounds that her hopes are likely to be thwarted, and lead only to disappointment and hardship for herself and her family.

It is considerations of this kind that make us unlikely to sympathize with Jenny's decision. We may (perhaps unjustifiably) imagine that Jenny's reasons are typical of women who choose twin reduction. This makes it hard to imagine sympathizing with any such decision. Moreover, even those of us who hold pro-choice views may think that a foetus is not just a clump of any-old cells, but that it deserves some degree of respect and deference in virtue of being a potential human person (even if not the full rights of an actual person). If so, it will seem that Jenny's mistaken assessment of her reasons led her to do something morally wrong in having an abortion. We may then worry that twin reduction can never be justified.

Yet we need not conclude from this that abortion is always and everywhere wrong, nor that it should be banned, nor even that the procedure of twin reduction specifically should be banned. To take an analogy: in standing up for the principle of freedom of expression, we endorse the principle that everyone should have a legal right to say what they will; in doing so we need not, of course, morally endorse the saying of everything that is in fact said. We stand for free expression not because we believe that every act of expression it permits is good or valuable or morally right, but because every alternative to that legal principle would be worse. Similarly, in the case of abortion, we can remain stalwart in our endorsement (perhaps limited by stage of pregnancy) of a woman's legal right to choose and a doctor's right to assist based on whichever reasons she sees fit, because we may reasonably think that every alternative principle for regulating abortion would be worse. We need not—and should not—assume that every woman's decision, for whatever reasons, to have an abortion is morally right. The questions of which abortions are right and of which principles for regulating abortions are right are separate questions, and neither pro-choice nor anti-abortion partisans should confuse them.

## Notes

1. <http://www.nytimes.com/2011/08/14/magazine/the-two-minus-one-preg nancy.html>
2. <http://jezebel.com/5830054/the-complicated-ethics-of-twin-reduction>
3. <http://www.slate.com/articles/health_and_science/human_nature/2011/08/ halfaborted.html>
4. <http://douthat.blogs.nytimes.com/2011/08/17/the-failure-of-liberal-bioethics/>

# 30

# NICK-LESS?

## Dominic Wilkinson

The American Academy of Pediatrics (AAP) has come under fire for a policy statement[1] that has a more nuanced approach to female circumcision than its previous absolute opposition. The new policy proposes that the law be changed to allow pediatricians to perform a ritual 'nick' as a compromise where families request female circumcision.

Female circumcision (also sometimes referred to as female genital mutilation) refers to procedures that intentionally alter or injure female genital tissue without a medical reason. It can include the partial or total removal of the clitoris or labia (the skin folds that surround the vagina), and/or the narrowing of the vaginal opening.

The AAP document strongly opposes all female circumcision that would lead to physical or psychological harm, but suggests that pricking or incising the skin of the external genitalia in females is less harmful than ear piercing. This proposal has led to outrage from groups who oppose female circumcision in all forms.

The AAP argues in favour of the ritual nick on several grounds:

> There is reason to believe that offering such a compromise may build trust between hospitals and immigrant communities, save some girls from undergoing disfiguring and life-threatening procedures in their native countries, and play a role in the eventual eradication of [female circumcision].

Opponents of the policy claim that allowing the compromise would undermine efforts to reduce far more harmful forms of female circumcision, and so lead to more mutilating forms of female circumcision. The authors of the AAP statement argue that the compromise would prevent at least some parents from going overseas to have far more extensive, risky, and harmful procedures (or having them illegally). It is hard to be sure what the overall effect of this more permissive policy would be. But the AAP statement is very clear that it does not condone any form of female circumcision, and that damaging forms of female circumcision should remain illegal. It appears plausible that allowing the ritual nick would prevent some harm.

However, Lakshmi Anantnarayam writing in *The Guardian*[2] claims that, even if the compromise were effective in reducing female circumcision, it should not be permitted: 'human rights standards are absolute and not to be compromised upon in the name of possible harm reduction'.

If all forms of female circumcision, including the suggested 'nick', represent serious human-rights violations, then perhaps it should not be allowed in any circumstances. But if the AAP authors are correct in their claim that there is no physical or psychological harm attributable to this procedure, how or why are the rights of the female child violated by having it performed? Their claim prompts another question. Why does the ritual nick violate the rights of females, but far more extensive genital surgery performed routinely on males not violate their rights? While there's no evidence that the ritual nick has any long-term effect, male circumcision involves removal of the foreskin, with potential impact on sexual functioning.[3]

Part of the motivation for the AAP's change of view appears to be recognition that its previous positions on male and female circumcision were inconsistent. There are two consistent positions:

A. Surgery on the genitals of the newborn for religious/cultural reasons or parental preference should not be permitted in either females or males.

B. Minor surgery, of an equivalent risk and extent, for religious/cultural reasons or parental preference should be permitted in both males and females.

The new statement from the AAP moves towards B, but does not achieve consistency. For that it would need to either permit more extensive genital cutting in females than the ritual nick (for example, excision of the clitoral hood), or prohibit excision of the foreskin in males (but allow a nicking or piercing of the foreskin). However, the

AAP offers a reasonable compromise, since there are some reasons to be more liberal about male than female circumcision.[4] The other point to note is that the AAP takes great pains to distinguish between interventions that should be discouraged, criticized, and avoided, and those that should be criminalized. Not all activities that are morally wrong should be legally prohibited. No parent *should* subject their child to medically unnecessary genital surgery in infancy. Ideally, if such procedures are culturally significant, they should be performed in later life when the individual can choose for themselves whether to undergo it. Circumcision procedures with significant risks of physical or psychological harm should be outlawed. Nevertheless, even if we disapprove, we may allow parents to choose minor low-risk forms of circumcision for their male or female infants.

## Notes

1. Committee on Bioethics (2010). 'Ritual genital cutting of female minors', *Pediatrics* 126/1: 191. <http://pediatrics.aappublications.org/cgi/content/full/125/5/1088>
2. Anantnarayan, L. (11 May 2010). 'Why are US doctors allowing genital mutilation?', *The Guardian*, Comment is Free. <http://www.guardian.co.uk/commentisfree/2010/may/11/female-genital-mutilation-us-nicking>
3. Earp, B. D. (2015). 'Do the benefits of male circumcision outweigh the risks? A critique of the proposed CDC guidelines', *Frontiers in Pediatrics* 3: 18. <http://journal.frontiersin.org/article/10.3389/fped.2015.00018/abstract>
4. Male circumcision (but not female) has some potential health benefits, offering a degree of protection against HIV. What's more, female circumcision, unlike the male form, includes a spectrum of far more pernicious forms, and often occurs within a social context of oppression, discrimination, and rights violations.

# 31

# PAEDOPHILIA AND PREDISPOSITION

## Kyle T. Edwards

There has been a flurry of newspaper articles considering 'the new science' of paedophilia. One, by Alan Zarembo, in the *Los Angeles Times* focused on the increasing consensus among researchers that paedophilia is a biological predisposition similar to heterosexuality or homosexuality.[1] Another, in *The Guardian*, quoted sources suggesting that perhaps some paedophilic relationships aren't all that harmful after all.[2] And the right-wing talk-show host, Rush Limbaugh, chimed in comparing the 'normalization' of paedophilia to the historical increase in the acceptance of homosexuality.[3]

So what's all the fuss about? Why does it matter for our moral appraisal of paedophiles whether paedophilia is innate or acquired? If we say that we can't 'blame' paedophiles for their attraction to children because they were 'born this way', is it problematic to condemn individuals for acting upon these (and other harmful) desires if it can be shown that poor impulse control is similarly genetically predisposed?

## Sexual orientation?

A good place to start is the controversy over whether or not paedophilia should be defined as a sexual orientation akin to heterosexuality and homosexuality. In other words, why does it matter how we label it?

In his article, Zarembo notes: 'Like many forms of sexual deviance, paedophilia once was thought to stem from psychological influences early in life. Now, many experts view it as a sexual orientation as immutable as heterosexuality or homosexuality. It is a deep-rooted predisposition—limited almost entirely to men—that becomes clear during puberty and does not change.' Like many, Zarembo implicitly links sexual orientation and immutability; paedophilia, this argument goes, ought to be seen as a sexual orientation precisely because it is unchangeable. It's far from clear, however, how this would alter our understanding of the morality of being sexually attracted to children. Presumably, if paedophilia were based on psychological influences early in life, we might attempt more early childhood interventions, but it wouldn't make any more sense to blame paedophiles for their early environment and upbringing than for their biological predisposition: either way it is out of their control.

Rush Limbaugh and some other members of the religious right have argued that recognizing paedophilia as a sexual orientation will have the same result as the relatively recent recognition of homosexuality as a sexual orientation: it will become more acceptable to act upon those sexual desires. This logic seems obviously confused. The reason we think that homosexual intercourse is morally acceptable (and was before society recognized it as so) is the understanding that it is a consensual act, not because it follows from an innate orientation rather than an acquired desire. Similarly, it would be odd to think that having sex with a child is wrong because paedophilia is an acquired rather than an innate attraction; we think it is wrong because children are not capable of consenting to sex due largely to their underdeveloped reasoning and decision-making capacities. (This, at least partially, seems to explain why you might have more trouble judging the actions of an adult who has sex with a 17-year-old than an adult who has sex with an 8-year-old; a 17-year-old hovers around the point at which we think he can make this decision for himself.) Having sex with a child, then, will be wrong regardless of whether or not the underlying attraction is deeply rooted in the offender's biology.

Thus, recognizing as a society that certain individuals are attracted to children does not imply that we condone *acting upon* these desires. What it does imply is that attempting to alter such individuals' desires is like trying to stop a heterosexual man from being attracted to women: it won't be very productive. It implies that a better method for preventing child molestation is focusing on behaviour—both by getting paedophiles to empathize with the physical and psychological harm a child would experience if molested, and by helping them to identify and exercise control over those types of situations in which their desires are most pronounced.

## Predisposition and impulse control

In 2005, in an attempt to convince self-identified paedophiles to seek help controlling their behaviour, researchers in Germany ran advertisements that read: 'You are not guilty because of your sexual desire, but you are responsible for your sexual behaviour.'[4] Similarly, James Cantor—the oft-cited researcher in recent news stories whose work suggests the biological component of paedophilia—has said: 'Not being able to choose your sexual interests doesn't mean you can't choose what you do.'[5] And perhaps the strongest take-away message from the host of recent news articles is that we cannot equate 'paedophile' with 'child molester'. All these claims suggest that just because some individuals are attracted to children does not mean that they will actually act upon these desires.

Contained within the first half of this type of argument is the almost always implicit suggestion that because paedophiles don't 'choose' to be attracted to children, because they are 'born that way', or because 'it's in their genes', we ought not to blame or fault them for what most people consider to be an appalling desire. This strikes many people as right—we can't blame people for what they can't control. The second half of the argument seems to be the other side of that equation—we can blame people for what they can control. Although paedophiles can't choose their desires, they can choose not to act upon them, and it is this behaviour for which we can hold them 'responsible'.

However, what if future studies show that impulse control has a more substantial genetic component than we currently think it does? What if some individuals have a significantly greater difficulty suppressing behaviour based upon harmful desires? Such individuals would not have chosen to have below average impulse control. Some might even express overwhelming grief at not being better able to control their behaviour. Do we still 'blame' them, are they still 'guilty', if they fail to suppress their desires and instead act upon them?[6]

We would be justified in imprisoning or institutionalizing them for such an act to prevent them from harming others. But the other justifications for punishment—retribution, rehabilitation, and deterrence—don't apply very well. By definition, a prison sentence couldn't deter an individual from doing something he *can't* stop himself from doing and rehabilitation could not change an *immutable* characteristic. Retribution would be even more problematically incoherent: we believe that a person must be *able* to do what he *ought* to do. Our concepts of crime and justice rest largely upon a belief that, when we do bad things, we could always have chosen to do otherwise. If so, the discovery of a significant genetic component to impulse control might be the point at which arguments about fairness cease to make sense within our current legal–moral framework: some people will do bad things because they were unluckily born less able to control their impulses than others.

# Notes

1. Zarembo, Alan (14 January 2013). 'Many researchers taking a different view of pedophilia', *Los Angeles Times*. <http://articles.latimes.com/2013/jan/14/local/la-me-pedophiles-20130115> last accessed 3 September 2015.
2. Henley, John (3 January 2013). 'Paedophilia: bringing dark desires to light', *The Guardian*, Society Section. <http://www.theguardian.com/society/2013/jan/03/paedophilia-bringing-dark-desires-light> last accessed 3 September 2015.
3. Limbaugh, Rush (7 January 2013). 'Don't pooh-pooh the Left's push to normalize pedophilia', *The Rush Limbaugh Show*, published transcript. <http://www.rushlimbaugh.com/daily/2013/01/07/don_t_pooh_pooh_the_left_s_push_to_normalize_pedophilia> last accessed 3 September 2015.
4. See Zarembo, note 1.
5. *BBC News* (28 November 2007). 'Brain wiring link to paedophilia'. <http://news.bbc.co.uk/2/hi/health/7116506.stm> last accessed 3 September 2015.
6. Note that this impulse control problem applies to all desires that would have harmful consequences if acted upon; it has no special relationship to paedophilia.

# 32

# CHECKING PEOPLE OUT

Ole Martin Moen

You're walking down the street. Approaching in the opposite direction you see a very attractive person. As he or she passes, you feel tempted to turn your head so as to, well, check them out. I assume that you have felt this temptation. I, at least, have felt it many times. I have resisted turning my head, however, since doing so is supposedly *a bad thing*.

But what, exactly, is supposed to make it bad?

One answer might be that it is a privacy invasion. But that can't be right. By turning your head, you don't come to see anything that isn't already public. The perspective that you get is identical to the perspective available to whoever is already walking behind the person.

A slightly different answer might be that you 'make use' of another person without their consent. After all, when checking somebody out, head-turners don't ask for permission. But this response is no more convincing. We don't think that looking at someone on the street for a few seconds requires their consent.

A third answer might be that, by turning your head to check someone out, you *objectify* them: you treat them not as the full person that they are, but as a bodily object for your personal gratification. And objectification, we are always told, is *bad*.

Much has been written about objectification, but a few points are worth making. First, it is a mundane—but seldom emphasized—fact that human beings are, in fact, objects, and in that sense similar to spoons, stars, and satsumas. Admittedly, we humans belong to a subcategory of objects that are *also* subjects, but that does not contradict the reality that we really are objects (if you are in doubt, locate a mirror). Accordingly, if we treat someone as an object, we are not treating them as something that they are not; we are treating them in accordance with just one of their aspects.

Treating someone on the basis of just one of their aspects *can* be bad. It is certainly bad in cases where they are harmed as a result. If I tread on your toe so as to reach for a book on a shelf, I treat you merely as an object having no valid interest in not being stepped on. I disregard your subjectivity and harm you as a result. But is a selective focus on just one aspect of a person problematic even in cases where it does not affect that person's well-being?

It might be suggested that checking somebody out somehow *reduces* them to one aspect (their physical attractiveness). But I don't understand what 'reducing' can mean in this context. In one sense of the term, I am often 'reduced' to one of my aspects. For example, I am *counted*—I was counted during registration at school, I am counted in the census. When I am counted I am reduced to a quantity or a number. Sometimes I am weighed. And sometimes I am registered as a citizen. But does any of this *reduce* me in a problematic manner? Does it deny that I have aspects other than a quantity, a weight, and a citizenship? I don't see why it should; it is only a selective focus on one of my aspects for a purpose where the other aspects are not so relevant. Equally, it is unclear why focusing on someone's body implies a rejection of the fact that the person has many other aspects.

There is, however, at least one plausible reason for why checking people out on the street is wrong. By checking somebody out one might make the other person annoyed, uncomfortable, and afraid. This *harm-based* argument certainly counts against many forms of checking people out.

Let me therefore propose a rule: *wait until the person is at least one full step behind you before you turn your head.* That way, they are very unlikely to notice that you are looking, and as long as they do not notice, they won't feel uncomfortable, afraid, or annoyed. (Of course, they might also turn their head to look at you, and then notice you checking them out. But this could result in a happy ending.)

One worry about my rule might be that others on the street could still see what was going on. Yet why should that matter? If we grant that the action itself is acceptable, it is puzzling that it could be made unacceptable by a bystander observing it.

Granted, there are many wrong ways to check people out. And it's not just that one's behaviour might be annoying or threatening. It might manifest a negative view of women (or men). When we are providing an ethical assessment of an activity, however, the interesting question is not whether there are *bad* ways of engaging in that activity. For there are bad ways of engaging in virtually any activity. The much more interesting question is whether there are *acceptable* ways of doing it.

I contend that there are no general reasons for why it is bad to turn one's head to check someone out on the street. Although there might be good reasons to avoid doing so in many contexts (if it would upset one's fiancée, say), occasionally catching a discreet glance over one's shoulder can be morally just fine.

Just remember the one-step rule.[1]

## Note

1. For further reading, see Papadaki, L. (2010). 'What is objectification?', *Journal of Moral Philosophy* 7: 16.

# 33

# FEMALE PHILOSOPHERS AND
# SEXUAL HARASSMENT

David Edmonds

I've been reading, for a research project, about a group of remarkable philosophers who were educated in Oxford during and after World War II: some went on to teach at Oxford. They include Elizabeth Anscombe, Philippa Foot, Mary Midgley, Iris Murdoch, and Mary Warnock.

Several of them, it transpires, were taught classics by a brilliant and charismatic professor, Eduard Fraenkel. In addition to imparting lessons to his female students about Aeschylus's *Agamemnon*, he would engage in what nowadays we would describe as egregious cases of sexual harassment.

What's strange is how little psychological impact his behaviour seems to have had on the young women he pawed over. Warnock writes that she had never 'after the beginning, seriously minded his advances ... the impropriety of his sexual behaviour seemed utterly trivial compared with the riches he offered us.'[1] Iris Murdoch concurred. Just imagine a female student today bracketing this point, 'Professor Grope was a first-rate teacher (though it's true that each week he tried to put his hand up my skirt) ...'.

The philosopher Miranda Fricker[2] argues that where an invidious attitude or practice is widespread, those guilty of having such an attitude or engaging in such a practice should not be held as blameworthy as they ought to be if the attitude or practice were (correctly and widely) seen as morally unacceptable. Thus we are not to hold the chauvinist pig or sexual harasser or casual racist of 1951 to the same standards as the chauvinist pig or sexual harasser or casual racist of 2016.

Perhaps the philosophers I've been reading about were failing to recall their true feelings of Fraenkel accurately. Or perhaps they were more damaged than they realized. Or maybe these gifted and academically successful thinkers were not representative of his other victims. Warnock mentions one student for whom the effect seems to have been deep and long-lasting.

But there's another interpretation.

Moral norms are ethical practices, ways of living, which are widely accepted in society. The evolution, in the right direction, of a moral norm will, hopefully, have the huge beneficial impact of reducing the number of violations of that norm. When it's generally regarded as inappropriate for a professor to make sexual advances to a student, there will be fewer professors who do it. But, perversely, it's possible that, at a time when such behaviour was so much more commonplace, students felt less violated by it than they would today.

There are two types of harm. If a friend betrays us we are harmed, even if we never discover the betrayal. This is a type of objective harm. Then there are subjective (psychological) harms. Altering some social norms might have the unwelcome consequence that when a violation of the norm occurs, the subjective harm might be all the greater.

That, of course, is not a good reason to stymie moral progress. But the degree to which victims are mentally scarred has implications in many areas—such as what support mechanisms for victims should be established, and what compensation is appropriate.

This line of thought also suggests that, in one way at least, a racist or sexist act or remark in 2016 is worse than it was in 1951. The appropriate sanction for the culprit should be adjusted accordingly.

## Notes

1. See Warnock, M. (2002). *A Memoir—People & Places* (Duckbacks), pp. 74–81.
2. <http://philosophybites.com/2008/03/miranda-fricker.html>

# 34

# AN UNFORTUNATE STATE
# OF AFFAIRS

## Hilary Greaves

Ashley Madison is an online extramarital dating service, running with the succinct subtitle 'Life is short. Have an affair.' On 20 July 2015 the service announced that hackers had breached its data security defences[1] and obtained identifying details for the site's 37 million members. In the months that have since past, the newspapers have reported case after case of divorce,[2] blackmail,[3] and, tragically, suicide.[4]

Reactions to the Ashley Madison scandal have been many and various, ranging from unreserved sympathy for the 'victims' to the view that subscribers to Ashley Madison were stupid and 'therefore' deserve everything they get. My own reaction to any case of family trauma caused by infidelity is rather one of sadness: the sadness of witnessing suffering that seems, in many or most cases, so eminently *avoidable*.

I do not mean that the suffering would have been avoided if the straying parties had kept strictly to their vows of monogamy, true though that may be. What strikes me most is rather the frequency of the refrain that what really hurt the wronged partner was 'not the sex, but the betrayal of trust'. This raises the urgent question of why the vows of monogamy were made in the first place. Of course, *once a promise is made,* (a) it should be kept and (b) one feels cheated, even humiliated, if one is on the receiving end of a promise-breaking; but those observations imply nothing about which promises are good ones to make. If one's partner really, really likes strawberries, to the point at which he or she would find them a source of great temptation if they became forbidden fruit, it would be a bad idea to make one's relationship conditional on an oath of strawberry abstinence, and then to be torn apart by the betrayal of trust when said oath is inevitably broken. The advocate of monogamy should take a long, hard look at whether the arguments for insisting on sexual abstinence are any stronger than the arguments for insisting on strawberry abstinence.

Sexual exclusivity is not the only way. In a relationship in which, for example, it is understood that this is one's primary relationship for the foreseeable future, but that either or both partners may legitimately desire and have sexual relations with others, there is no reason to feel 'cheated' if indeed such additional sexual relations occur. In another model, successfully adhered to by a significant minority, a household might consist of multiple men and multiple women, where each household member has relationships with two or more other household members, on equal footings, and children might have any biologically possible combination of parents. Far from being a hell of intrigue and suspicion, if asked to describe the nature of their relationships to outsiders, people actually in such polyamorous relationships tend to place *more* emphasis on honesty, open communication, and trust than those in monogamous relationships. Polyamory is not for everyone, but its existence does lend additional credence to the idea that it is trust that is really the key to a relationship, rather than sexual exclusivity *per se*.

Some advocates of monogamy think that no such alternative arrangement could be stable. Husbands and wives of many years, they worry, would be torn apart by the ever-shifting process of following their sexual inclinations and romantic whims; the value of long-term shared experience and commitment would be pushed into the background, and we would all end up alone and isolated. But experience belies these claims and, for better or worse, neither does the data on divorce rates in supposedly monogamous societies support the claim that a system of monogamy is any more conducive to long-term stability.

It is also instructive to recall that most of us succumb to an urge towards exclusivity in the domain of *friendship* when we are children. In my primary school and early high school years, all but the most unfortunate girls in the class had a 'best friend'. Any excessive degree of favouritism towards another—say, giggling and whispering with a girl who was not one's current best friend and refusing to share the secret with the chosen one—was a serious business, and the occasional actual rearrangement of the best-friend partnerships were matters of minor trauma. We have since grown out of this infantile insistence in the case of friendships, and we would have no truck with arguments that this was a mistake. The advocate of monogamy should take a long, hard look at whether the arguments for insisting on exclusivity of sexual relationships are any stronger than the arguments for insisting on exclusivity of friendships.

Some advocates of monogamy insist that once in a committed relationship, one *should not desire* sexual relations with anybody else. In the ideal case, they say, one's chosen partner is the ultimate focus of one's desire and provides for all one's needs and tastes, so there is no need to look elsewhere. This is not a particularly convincing claim (again, it seems no more plausible than the analogous and highly dubious claim regarding friendship), but even if true, it is irrelevant. Our question is what the norms of relationships should be, *given* the tendencies and desires that we actually have, not which tendencies or desires we 'should' have; a matter that is anyway largely beyond our control.

The monogamy-monger's final argument is usually an appeal to some sort of biological necessity: as irrational as it may be, they say, humans are just biologically hard-wired to feel anxiety and jealousy if a sexual partner also has other sexual partners. Those who try to escape the mould of monogamy, according to this final argument, are attempting to fly in the face of their biological destiny, and are doomed to failure.

The core 'hard-wiring' claim in this argument may or may not be true, as a matter of biology. Certainly, it is easy to think of evolutionary-style explanations of why it might be true: evolutionary ancestors who fought off or even killed their sexual rivals were, perhaps, more likely to pass on their genes than would-be ancestors who did not. (Equally certainly, there are some thoroughly non-monogamous species, and they evolved too; but let that pass.) Even if the hard-wiring claim is accepted, though, it does not follow that we should institute a rule of monogamy in our relationships. First, the fact that some *tendency* is inbuilt does not mean that we cannot overcome it; it does not mean that we have to *actually feel* jealousy. We probably all have some inbuilt tendency to seek out fatty foods, but that does not mean that one cannot get oneself, through habituation and reflection, into a state in which one's reactions to such foods are ones of indifference or even repulsion. And, second, the fact, if it does remain a fact, that one feels some jealousy does not mean that one has to bow to it, instead of dismissing it as an irrationality, a defect. Many of the factors that might once have made monogamy adaptive are anyway no longer applicable in the modern world: contraception can largely prevent the creation of undesired offspring from extra-pair copulations, and DNA testing can establish paternity in case this is in doubt. We may balk at allowing such an outdated evolutionary inheritance to keep us prisoner.

The users of Ashley Madison were acting on the basis of urges they could not help feeling, desires they could not help having. In some distant possible world, all relationships permit open acknowledgement of the participants' desires, and permit, nay encourage, explorations of harmless opportunities for the enrichment of life. In that world, the Ashley Madison hackers have no power to cause even a sleepless night.

## Notes

1. <https://en.wikipedia.org/wiki/Ashley_Madison_data_breach>
2. <http://www.dailymail.co.uk/news/article-3206003/Wife-starts-Ashley-Madison-divorce-proceedings-lawyers-call-hack-Black-Friday-say-s-like-Christmas-September.html?>
3. <http://www.skynews.com.au/news/national/2015/10/13/ashley-madison-blackmail-scam.html>
4. <http://www.dailymail.co.uk/news/article-3227253/Pastor-seminary-teacher-outed-member-Ashley-Madison-commits-suicide-carried-shame.html>

# SPORT

# 35

# SPORT HATRED

## Joshua Shepherd

Fans of Auburn University's football team used to gather after victories at Toomer's corner in Auburn, Alabama, to throw rolls of toilet paper into the historic oak trees there. The trees have been removed. Not because Auburn University wanted it that way: Harvey Updyke, a fan of the University of Alabama's football team—Auburn's hated cross-state rival—poisoned the trees in 2010. Updyke was caught when he called in to a local sports radio show to brag about the deed. He was charged with criminal mischief, desecrating a venerated object, and damaging agriculture. He served six months in jail and was released in June of 2013.[1]

This is, of course, a bad situation. I've been to football games at Auburn, and though I sport-hate their football team, the celebration at Toomer's corner was a great tradition and the trees, themselves, were beautiful. I don't wish to pass more judgement on Updyke, but rather to reflect on an ethical question his action raises.

Allow me a stipulation: Updyke's crime was motivated by a particular kind of hatred. This is a kind of hatred often sanctioned in America and most Western societies. Call it *sport-hatred*. I understand hatred to be a package of intense blame-related emotions and behavioural dispositions directed at people, objects, ideas, symbols, actions. In turn, I understand sport-hatred as hatred in the context of sports. Typically, sport-hate is directed at players, teams, organizations, mascots, and so on. When you sport-hate some agent, you hate them because of their role or behaviour in the context of some sport.

Thus understood, sport-hatred will play a role in one's life—will motivate actions, will bleed into one's other emotions and activities—roughly to the extent that sport plays a role in one's life. It is possible for sport-hatred to cross boundaries, influencing one's behaviour quite broadly. It is often said that Magic Johnson and Isaiah Thomas—both hall-of-fame NBA players—were close friends until they met in the NBA finals. Allegedly, the competition was so intense that their friendship cooled for years afterwards. Much more extreme than this, in 2013 one fan of Alabama's football team is said to have killed another fan for not expressing enough sorrow over the team's recent loss.[2]

So, though it is true that some expressions of sport-hatred are theatrical and constrained within the confines of some particular game or sporting event, this is not generally the case. Sport-hatred is hatred in the context of some sport, but the boundaries of sport-hatred are as blurry as the boundaries between sport and the rest of life. For some passionate fans, this boundary is quite blurry indeed.

The question that interests me is this: is sport-hatred morally permissible?

Obviously Updyke's crime crossed moral boundaries. I am not asking about the moral permissibility of all actions motivated by sport-hatred. I am asking whether sport-hatred itself is morally permissible: do those of us who frequently undergo strong bouts of sport-hatred exhibit a moral defect? Am I morally blameworthy because I hate (citing teams here to avoid naming names) Arsenal, Duke University's basketball team, or the Philadelphia Eagles?

Hatred itself is rarely, if ever, praiseworthy. Sport-hatred, by contrast, is an oft-celebrated phenomenon. *Forbes Magazine* annually publishes a 'top ten' list of the most disliked athletes. The sports and pop-culture bellwether *Grantland* recently hosted a vote to determine the most hated college basketball player of the last 30 years. Thousands of readers voted to winnow a field of 32 down to the most hated one.[3] If sport-hatred is morally wrong, it is the most widely celebrated moral violation in modern society.

In an interesting discussion, Peter Arnold mentions three possible views on the relation between sport and morality.[4] First, sport is morally valuable in the sense that sport constitutes a kind of moral training ground. Second, sport is morally neutral, or at least morally unimportant. As Arnold describes this view, sport is 'essentially non-serious'. Third, sport is morally disvaluable in the sense that the kinds of character traits and actions promoted by desires to succeed in sport—for example, aggression, dominance over others—are morally onerous.

Of course there are more possible views than these, and it is implausible to think that sport is essentially morally valuable, neutral, or disvaluable, rather than a mixture of all three. Sometimes engagement in a sport does serve to cultivate the moral virtues; certainly, many place their children onto sports teams not just because they want them to have fun and make friends, but because they want them to learn the value of hard work, cooperation, and so on. But most of us are familiar with examples of sport-vices: little league coaches who care only about winning or selfish players who seek only personal glory. And many of us feel the pull of the sport-is-neutral view. What's so bad about a bit of vicious banter in the context of a game? Isn't following a team much more fun when you hate your rivals?

I want to say that sport-hatred is permissible, under certain conditions. But it is sometimes impermissible.

An example of unjustified sport-hatred: we might cheer when an opposing player is injured.

An example of justified sport-hatred: famously, the New England patriots were once caught spying on the play-calling of other teams, giving them an unfair advantage. It is justified to sport-hate them for that.

Considerations of proportionality are relevant here. It is possible to sport-hate someone too much. The sport-hate heaped on LeBron James, for example, was perhaps initially justified: LeBron callously left his home-town Cleveland Cavaliers for perceived quick success with the Miami Heat. Fans burned James's jerseys. The media loved the spectacle. But the sport-hatred continued, and to some extent still continues, years later. This is odd, since LeBron is in many ways an excellent teammate and competitor. The sport-hatred many still heap upon LeBron is out of proportion.

This discussion suggests that the *reasons* we engage in sport-hatred (as participants and observers) are crucial. What we need to identify, then, are the kinds of reasons that justify sport-hatred.

My proposal is this: the kinds of reasons that justify sport-hatred *mirror* those that justify hatred outside of sport.

We have to be careful here. The field of play is not entirely morally neutral. Some players can exhibit morally vicious character traits in the midst of a game. This happens sometimes if a player delivers a vicious foul on another (think of Zinedine Zidane's World Cup Final head-butt).

At other times, it happens more systematically. Notably, one of the most hated college basketball players in recent memory, J.J. Redick, has admitted as much. In an article discussing the amount of vitriol Redick received while playing for Duke, Redick is quoted as saying: 'I probably deserved it. I was sort of a prick.'[5] In such cases, we might be justified in blaming the person even outside the context of the game. By contrast, the kind of thing I am describing here involves sport-hatred that is justified only within the context of the sport.

What I would like to suggest is that justifying reasons for sport-hatred not only track those that justify non-sport-hatred, but might mirror these reasons. I take this to be an importantly different relation, one in which we respond, not to features that themselves justify hatred, but to features that meet a *mirroring* requirement. To understand what I have in mind here, note that sport competitions often mirror real-life moral conflicts. Many of the best sports movies—*Mighty Ducks, Rocky IV, Karate Kid*—capitalize on this fact, offering us a moral and a sports conflict that mirror and play off each other in obvious ways. Consider two examples of how sport-hatred can mirror morally justified hatred in non-sport contexts.

First, it is sometimes the case that we come to sport-hate a player for certain character-related failings. That is, we heap blame and scorn upon a player for consistently failing to meet some norm *internal to the sport*. This might be a failure to rotate on defence, a failure to wrap up a tackle, a failure to make an easy shot, or whatever. It would be odd to suspect that some person's deficiencies in a sport are easily transmitted to non-sports contexts (in spite of John Wooden's famous quote that sports 'reveal character'). In my view it is justified to sport-hate such a person because, by the standards internal to that sport (or to sports in general), their character is deficient.

Second, we sometimes come to sport-hate a player or a team because we find their success an example of unfairness. Many people loathe the New York Yankees because it seems to them that the Yankees can simply buy success. Their success seems undeserved, and the sport-hate is motivated by a justified hatred of unfairness.

When our reasons for sport-hating mirror justified reasons for hating outside the context of sports, we are justified in sport-hating that person, team, or whatever. That such reasons tend to arise more often in sport than outside of it reveals something interesting about sport in general. As Arnauld argues, sport often serves as a kind of moral training ground; a place where some of the stronger emotions can be (relatively) safely experienced and expressed. Without contexts such as sport, we would have to develop a facility with such strong emotions on the fly, in 'real life'. That we have a chance to express sport-hatred in a relatively safe context is, arguably, a good thing, even when the sport-hatred is impermissible. It is even better when, as is often the case, the sport-hatred is justified.

## Notes

1. <http://espn.go.com/college-football/story/_/id/9360611/harvey-updyke-freed-ending-toomer-corner-tree-poisoning-case>
2. <http://www.usatoday.com/story/sports/ncaaf/2013/12/02/deadly-shooting-over-alabama-loss-to-auburn/3819905/>
3. <http://grantland.com/features/a-tournament-determine-most-hated-college-basketball-players-last-30-years/>
4. Arnold, P.J. (1994). 'Sport and moral education', *Journal of Moral Education* 23/1: 75–89.
5. Mays, R. (14 March 2013). '"I was sort of a prick": J.J. Redick on playing "J.J. Redick"', *Grantland*. <http://www.grantland.com/blog/the-triangle/post/_/id/54296/i-was-sort-of-a-prick-j-j-redick-on-playing-j-j-redick> last accessed 3 November 2013.

# 36

# DOPING

*When will we learn?*

Julian Savulescu

Soon after the London Olympics, the second fastest runner of all time, the US's Tyson Gay, tested positive for a banned substance,[1] along with the Jamaican sprinters Asafa Powell and Sherone Simpson, making for shocked headlines across the world. Gay and Powell were both finalists in the men's 100 metre race. Two further members of the eight-man line-up, Justin Gaitlin and Yohan Blake, had previously received doping bans.

But this is just one high-profile story amongst a recent rash of similar sports stories. In athletics, 24 Turkish athletes were confirmed to have tested positive;[2] Australian Rules Football is still reeling from the ongoing Essendon scandal, which was proven to involve at least one substance subsequently approved by the US Food and Drug Administration (FDA) as a food supplement;[3] and over in the US, there was an inquiry into an anti-ageing laboratory said to supply human growth hormone to top baseball players.[4] Whilst the 100th Tour de France was untainted by major positive tests, cycling doping cases continued with two Giro d'Italia riders testing positive.[5]

## The failure of zero tolerance

We don't know which individuals are doping and which are not. One thing we do know is that the zero tolerance ban on doping has failed.

The 'War on Doping' has seen several false victories. In 2000 the first tests for erythropoietin (EPO)—which boosts the oxygen-carrying capacity of blood—were introduced. In 2007 Pat McQuaid, head of UCI, declared biological passports 'a new and historic step in the fight against doping'.[6] Autologous blood tests were all but announced for the 2012 Olympics, but at the time of writing have not yet been implemented. The science of drug testing has progressed, but it appears that the dopers are a step ahead.

Lance Armstrong is a case in point. He was tested in and out of competition, before and after EPO tests were implemented, before and after biological passports were introduced. Yet he was only caught through the forced testimony of his teammates, who turned him in for the chance to continue their own careers as confessed dopers, many of them still riding at the elite, professional level.

The decision of a Spanish court to destroy evidence from Eufemiano Fuentes's trial means that we may never know who was involved with that particular clinic, but it is thought to include clients from athletics, tennis, and football as well as cyclists. Fuentes was arguably the greatest doping doctor in cycling.[7]

Time and again we are told the culture has changed. But the doping cases keep coming and performances keep improving. The 2012 Olympics saw 66 Olympic records and 30 world records broken. One obvious question is, if athletes can continue to break records without doping, why do they dope, with the penalties involved?

## The limits of human physiology

We reached the limits of human performance in sprinting about 20 years ago. Only seven men have broken 9.8 seconds in the 100 metre sprint. Of these, four have received bans for failed tests during their career. A fifth, Maurice Greene, was named by *The New York Times* as a client of former discus thrower and confessed drug dealer Angel Guillermo Heredia, paying $10,000 to purchase performance-enhancing drugs. Greene admitted the payment, but denied it was for drugs. To keep improving, to keep beating records, to continue to train at the peak of fitness, to recover from the injury that training inflicts, we need enhanced physiology. Spectators and sponsors want faster times and broken records, and thus so do athletes. They all want rapid recovery from injury after grueling training and competition schedules. We have exhausted the human potential.

Is it wrong to aim for zero tolerance and performances that are within natural human limits? No, but it is not enforceable. It is not realistic.

## Some counterarguments

The strongest argument against doping is safety. The harm inflicted on East German athletes in the 1970s must never be repeated.[8] But anything is dangerous if taken to excess. Water will kill you if you drink enough. As sport has shown over the last 20 years, performance enhancers can be administered safely. They could be administered yet more safely if it was brought out into the open.

Of course, there is no such thing as risk-free sport. But we need a balance between safety, enforceability, and spectacle. Elite sport is fundamentally unsafe. Manchester United's footballers suffered 68 injuries in the 2014–15 season. In the US a settlement is underway to compensate American Football players who have suffered from concussions sustained over the course of their careers. In 2003 helmets were made mandatory by the cycling federation, UCI, following the death of Andrei Kivilev. It was entirely appropriate to enforce the wearing of helmets to limit the safety risks. But it would be inappropriate to limit the race to only straight, wide roads, or to remove downhill racing, or to take any number of other measures that would increase safety but ruin the sport as a spectacle and as a cultural practice. It would be a waste of time to take other measures, such as limiting the amount of time that riders can train, even on the grounds of safety. It could not be enforced.

Enforceability requires reasonable limits. If we set the maximum speed limit for cars at 20 mph, it would be safer. Many of the people who died on the roads would have been saved. But more people would speed. Speed is risky, but it is also pleasurable, benefits the economy, and is convenient. You have to weigh the benefits and harms, and draw a reasonable, enforceable line.

A second good objection lies in the nature of the intervention. If a substance came to dominate a sport or override the value of the sport, that would be a good reason to ban it. For example, it should be impermissible to give a substance to boxers so that they felt no fear, or to archers so that they had rock-steady hands. But a substance that allows safer, faster recovery from training, or from injury, does not interfere with sport.

We are confused and often emotional about doping. Drugs bring to mind substances like ecstasy or cocaine or heroin. But most doping today uses natural substances that are involved in normal human physiology and vary from time to time and person to person. Testosterone, blood, and growth hormone are all endogenous substances (which occur naturally within the body) and are banned, while drugs such as caffeine are exogenous (not naturally occurring in the body, and effective in increasing performance) and are allowed. Taking the drug EPO increases the amount of red blood cells (hematocrit levels), and is banned. Sleeping in a hypoxic air tent has the same effect, but is perfectly legal.

Athletes are using these substances to optimize their own physiology, just as they do with diet, trying to maximize fluids and glucose at the right times. Confessed doping cyclist Tyler Hamilton claims in his book, *The Secret Race*, to have lost a race due to failing to take a 100 calorie energy gel at the correct time (despite the fact that he was also doping).

All of these variables are themselves affected by training. Over the course of the Tour de France, a cyclist would lose their natural levels of red blood cells from the immense effort. The training period before the race is about optimizing human physiology. Improvements can be made through a careful attention to diet to influence the availability of glucose and water, or by taking EPO in order to increase the availability of oxygen.

The risks of doping have been overstated, and zero-tolerance represents the kind of unreasonable limit that is destined to be ignored by athletes. It is time to rethink the absolute ban and instead to pick limits that are safe and enforceable.

# Notes

1. <http://www.guardian.co.uk/sport/2013/jul/14/tyson-gay-tests-positive-banned-substance>
2. <http://www.reuters.com/article/2013/06/28/us-athletics-turkey-doping-idUSBRE95R0KP20130628>
3. <http://www.heraldsun.com.au/sport/afl/world-anti-doping-boss-lays-down-law-to-crisis-hit-essendon-about-banned-substance-aod9604/story-fni5f220-1226669739324>
4. <http://www.theglobeandmail.com/sports/baseball/a-rod-meets-with-major-league-baseball-report/article13209075/>

5. <http://www.bbc.co.uk/sport/0/cycling/22652887>
6. <http://www.reuters.com/article/2007/10/23/us-cycling-doping-macquaid-idUSL237207320071023>
7. <http://www.dailymail.co.uk/sport/othersports/article-2317138/Eufemiano-Fuentes-given-year-suspended-sentence-blood-bags-destroyed.html>
8. <http://www.bbc.co.uk/sport/0/athletics/22269445>

# 37

# TENNIS AND SEX

## David Edmonds

Once a week I thrash around haplessly on the tennis court. This week, I'm also a tennis spectator. While the global economy implodes, at least one event appears to be untouched: the 2009 Australian Open. Rafael Nadal has netted the eye-watering AUD$2 million first prize for the men's single title. The women's champion, Serena Williams, has earned . . . well, exactly the same.[1]

After a long-running campaign by various groups, all the Grand Slam tennis tournaments now offer equal prize money to both sexes: Wimbledon fell into line in 2007. The argument was that just as no distinction should be made between women and men in the office, so there should be no distinction drawn on the tennis court.

But this is a very bad argument. The demand for equal pay in the workplace is that the reward system ought to be meritocratic and sex-blind. What matters is the quality and quantity of a person's output, not their sex.

The same argument cannot justify the cry for equal pay in sport. Put aside the fact that men play the best of five sets, women the best of three: this silly anachronism could and should easily be changed, grounded, as it is, on the erroneous notion that women have less stamina. But the whole point of dividing up the sexes in tennis is that the 'work', the 'output', the tennis, is not equal. On average, men are better than women at tennis and the top men are better than the top women. Strength and speed are both crucial factors determining tennis success and elite male tennis players are stronger and faster than elite female ones. If tennis did not have separate male and female sections, and awarded prize money on a sex-blind basis, men would win all (or almost all) of it.

So the comparison with the ordinary workplace is lazy and flawed. Now possibly a convincing case could be made for equal prize money. Once the categories—men's tennis, women's tennis—have been established, it could be argued that women's tennis is just as (if not more) entertaining, that just as many people want to watch, and so on. These are empirical claims which, combined with a normative claim (e.g. prize money should be a function of market demand) justify equalizing rewards once the sport has been split along sex lines. But they do not provide us with a reason for dividing the sport along these lines in the first place.

For that you need a different argument. And it's not clear how it would go. It might be said that if tennis were sex-blind, this would be unfair, for no woman would have a genuine shot at the Australian Open. Half the population would thereby be deprived of any genuine opportunity to acquire the status and riches that go with being a tennis champ. True enough. But in that regard women are only part of a group constituting almost the entire population, all of whom are denied sporting riches by innate athletic mediocrity. Why is it any more unjust that all tennis-talentless men be effectively excluded from glory? Should they not have their own tournament offering the same riches?

I write with feeling...

## Note

1. <http://tennis.sporting99.com/australian-open/prize-money.html>

# BRAINS

# 38

# MY BRAIN MADE ME DO IT—SO WHAT?

Walter Sinnott-Armstrong

VIJETH: Where were you? You promised to drive me to the airport, but you never showed up, and I missed my flight. You haven't even apologized. Why did you let me down?

FELIPE: I watched a movie instead. It was a romantic comedy. Don't be angry with me.

VIJETH: You watched a movie! What kind of excuse is that?

FELIPE: It's the newest kind, a neural excuse. I really wanted to watch the movie, and my desires are lodged in my brain, so my brain made me do it.

VIJETH: Of course your brain made you do it. It wasn't your foot or your stomach that made you do it. It was your desires, and your desires are located in your brain; so your brain caused you to do it.

FELIPE: Excellent, so we agree.

VIJETH: I agree that your brain made you do it, but that's irrelevant. What matters is *which part* of your brain made you do it. What made you do it was activations in those parts of your brain that constitute your desire to watch the movie. That is just a pseudo-scientific way of stating that your desires made you do it. But if you did it because of the brain states that constitute your desires, then—to put it another way—you did it because you wanted to! And, sorry, that's still no excuse.

FELIPE: You miss my point. My desires *made* me do it. After those desires were in place, given the situation, I *had* to watch the movie.

VIJETH: Maybe I did miss something. Did you struggle against your desires? Did you seriously think about picking me up, but then found yourself somehow overpowered by the appeal of watching the movie? Did the movie distract you, so that you simply forgot to pick me up?

FELIPE: No, none of that. I just found out that the movie was on television and decided to watch it.

VIJETH: Then you controlled your actions. If you had not wanted to watch it, you would not have watched it. Nobody and nothing outside you made you do it. Your brain—or at least the part that constitutes your desire to watch the movie—is part of you. It is not some alien invader. It is not like a tumour that grows against your will and can be cut out.[1] You have no basis for denying that your desires reflect who you are.

FELIPE: But something external created those desires. My parents loved romantic comedies and passed their passion on to me. I couldn't help but want to watch that movie. And, gee, it was good.

VIJETH: Don't blame your parents. You could still control how you acted.

FELIPE: Not really. In the precise circumstances, given all of my desires and beliefs, I would act in the same way every time.

VIJETH: Fine, but one factor in those circumstances is how much you care about me, right?

FELIPE: Sure.

VIJETH: And if you had cared more about me, you would have driven me to the airport before watching the movie. So what your excuse comes down to is that your brain did not include enough concern for me. How is that supposed to make me less enraged? Your brain does not care about me or you do not care about me. Either way, you treated me like dirt.

FELIPE: Please try to understand. I had no choice about how much I cared for you. Since my concerns determined my acts, I had no choice about how I acted.

VIJETH: No choice? You had a working car, and you remembered that I was counting on you. If you had chosen to keep your promise, then you would have kept it. So you did what you did because you chose to do that and not something else. If you deny that you had a choice, I don't know what you mean by a choice.

FELIPE: Okay, there was a choice, but I did not make it. My brain did.

VIJETH: Does that even make sense? Anyway, if your brain made the choice, and if the part of your brain that made the choice was the part that constitutes your desires, then that convoluted description just means that you chose to watch the movie because you wanted to watch it and didn't care enough about me.

FELIPE: I grant you that I made a choice. However, I had no real option, because my action was inevitable.

VIJETH: Again, what matters is not *that* it was inevitable but *what makes it* inevitable. The only things that made your choice inevitable were your desire to watch the movie and your lack of concern for me. It's not like you were pushed or threatened. What you did depended on your own desires and choices. Re-describing those mental states in terms of brain states does not change the crucial fact that you chose to watch the movie because you wanted to watch it more than you cared for me. I have every reason to be furious with you. This is not affected one iota by a pseudo-excuse, like 'My brain made me do it.'

FELIPE: I'm really sorry.

## Note

1. <http://www.ncbi.nlm.nih.gov/pubmed/12633158> and <http://abcnews.go.com/blogs/headlines/2012/01/lawmaker-steals-leather-pants-brain-tumor-may-be-responsible-lawyer-says/>

# 39

# MY CLIENT'S BRAIN
# IS TO BLAME

Simon Rippon

It seems like a platitude to say that criminals are justly punished only when they were under an obligation to obey a law, they violated the law, and they lack sufficient excuse. It follows that any justly punished criminal has failed to do what they ought. Even the most cool, calculating criminal has thus acted in error, in an important sense: a right-thinking person would not have done what they did. Still, many criminals can justly be held responsible. Or so we ordinarily think.

I came to doubt this familiar wisdom when I read a news report about a Californian politician named Mary who was caught shoplifting. Mary's lawyer claimed that her impaired judgement may have been caused by a benign brain tumour.[1]

Suppose that Mary's lawyer's explanation was true. We can easily accept that a brain tumour could undermine Mary's moral responsibility and excuse her criminal actions, because we know that tumours can press on parts of the brain and prevent them functioning properly, causing all kinds of unusual thoughts and behaviours. And Mary could hardly be held responsible for her having a brain tumour. She didn't choose to have it; it just happened to her.

But now imagine someone like Mary who never had a brain tumour—let's call her Nary. Imagine, though, that when Nary was prosecuted for shoplifting, her lawyer argued: 'My client's brain caused her action, and since my client didn't choose her brain, she isn't responsible.' That would strike most of us as an odd sort of defence. Why?

First, perhaps this sounds odd because we assume that Nary *is* her brain, thus rendering the suggestion that Nary's action was *caused* by her brain a kind of nonsense. I don't think this explanation is very plausible, though, because most of us clearly don't think that a normal person is less than two kilos in weight and enclosed within a bony skull.

As a second guess, maybe we think Nary is responsible for what her brain does because we think that Nary's brain is part of Nary, and that Nary is in control of what her brain does. But how is this possible? It seems more accurate to say that Nary's brain is in control of what Nary does. We might be in the grip of a dualistic picture of the mind according to which Nary herself is an immaterial mind or soul that has causal influence over her brain. But this theory is not scientifically plausible. It is hard to imagine what this immaterial substance could be, and how it could fit into and interact with the naturalistic universe. Many of us are convinced that dualism is false, yet it still seems obvious to us that Nary cannot be excused merely by showing that her brain caused her action.

Perhaps, thirdly, we reflect that all our actions are caused by our brains, and that we know that people are responsible for at least some of their actions. It follows that the fact that a person's brain caused her action cannot absolve her of responsibility.

But now consider what the brain is: it is, essentially, a biological machine; 100 billion nerve cells living in a chemical soup, firing electrical impulses at each other. And in years to come, as neuroscience improves and expands our knowledge of the brain, we may reach the stage where a defence lawyer like Nary's will be able to explain any particular criminal misjudgement as a result of this-or-that chemical overdose or deficit, this-or-that badly routed synapse, the growth of this-or-that cell, or—perhaps—this-or-that quantum random occurrence.

How will we respond to these hyper-medicalizing future lawyers, who blame all criminal behaviour on some minor malfunction or other in their clients' brains? What's the difference between the idea that this-or-that bit of your brain (albeit perhaps a microscopic bit) made you irrational, and the idea that a large tumour made you irrational? A tumour is not some alien invader: it is a proliferation of your own cells. Is it, then, physical size that matters here? Surely not!

It may be tempting to reply that brain tumours absolve people of responsibility only because they impinge on their *general* capacity to think and act rationally. Since most ordinary criminals retain the general capacity to think and act rationally, it is not unjust to hold them responsible, and to punish them.

But this reply misses the point. Imagine another hypothetical person, Henry, who has only one flaw: a tiny brain tumour that normally has no discernible effects. While Henry retains the *general* capacity to think and act rationally, let us suppose that his tiny brain tumour, by a particular fluke, caused Henry to judge that shoplifting was the thing to do while he was shopping at 2:54 pm on 1 August 2013 and led to his stealing some trousers. While Henry might well still be responsible for what he does *generally*, he seems no more responsible for *this* act than does Mary with her large judgement-impairing tumour. And if the tiny tumour can indeed excuse Henry's criminal misjudgement, then why not other flaws such as a synapse, or a cell, or whatever else in the brain that might lead to a failure to do what one ought?

One might think that normally brain tumours only excuse because they make criminal punishment ineffective: people whose tumours cause them to commit crimes simply can't be deterred like most other people. The problem with this thought is that it ignores the fact that, intuitively, the justification of punishment depends not just on its expected effects, but at least partly also on one's responsibility for choices one has already made. Suppose that in fact Mary's tumour did cause her action, but that, nevertheless, punishment would induce overwhelming fear that would deter her from repeating the crime. While this may give us a reason to punish her, it does not seem like a sufficient justification. After all, her action was outside her control! Shall we also pre-emptively punish the innocent, if doing so would deter crimes they have yet to commit?

It seems inconsistent, in principle, to accept the tumour excuse issued by Mary's lawyer, but not the other kinds of neurological excuse envisaged here. The odds are high that neuroscience will one day force us to give up the common-sense idea that many criminals can justly be held responsible for breaching the law.

## Note

1. <http://abcnews.go.com/blogs/headlines/2012/01/lawmaker-steals-leather-pants-brain-tumor-may-be-responsible-lawyer-says/>

# 40

# MAPPING BRAINS AND
# FINDING DIRECTION

Regina Rini

According to a recent report in *The New York Times*,[1] the US government will soon announce plans to fund the Brain Activity Map. Modelled on the highly successful Human Genome Project, the Brain Activity Map is an effort to identify functional networks of neurons, possibly leading to a full understanding of how mental processes like perception and memory are physically distributed in the brain. The scientific and medical potentials, perhaps including new treatment of conditions like schizophrenia or autism, are fantastic. By developing monitoring techniques like calcium imaging, nanoparticle sensor detection, or synthetic-DNA chemical recording, neuroscientists hope to be able to trace the paths travelled by our thoughts and memories. Yet before setting off on this cartographic adventure, perhaps we ought to first stop and remind ourselves where we already are.

In a 2012 *Neuron* paper[2] proposing the Brain Activity Map, a group of leading scientists briefly acknowledge some ethical worries, including 'issues of mind-control, discrimination, health disparities, unintended short- and long-term toxicities'. This is a reasonable, if somewhat eclectic, list of concerns. But I would like to add one more: brain-mapping, like gene-mapping, risks making us overconfident in our self-understanding. The better we come to understand our brains, the more tempting it will be to assume we understand ourselves.

Think for a moment about the history of major advances in human-directed science: Darwinism, psychoanalytics, behaviourism, sociobiology, cybernetics, genomics. With each progression has come a deluge of sweeping assertions about the new completeness of our self-understanding, followed later by a far quieter admission that whatever else we may be, we are also mysteries. In the worst moments, our fleeting certitude fuelled attempts to reorganize societies along purportedly scientific lines, from racist eugenics to disastrous Marxist utopianism. Even when spared catastrophic miscalculation, we've still suffered coarsening reductions in public debate about human nature, where hopes and commitments were temporarily reduced to the jargon of operant reinforcements or behavioural phenotypes.

The point here is not to deny the reality of scientific descriptions of humanity, nor to retreat into a neo-Romantic induced ignorance. The point is simply to sound a warning, to jot a note to ourselves in this relatively sober moment, before the allure of the scientifically novel begins to blindingly illuminate our horizons. The history of psychology shows that we are never content to take our experiences as subjectively given: the warmth of chewed peppers, the softness of a baby's palm, the stinging effervescence of failure. We seem to expect that we would better understand ourselves if only we could quantify our experiences, or locate them in space. We are never satisfied with the results. Yet maps are awesomely seductive bearers of information, so simply compact and so seemingly complete. Mapped brains will be more potent still, enfolding the vanity of portraiture in the certainty of topography.

I'm aware that what I am articulating is not so much an argument as an anxiety. I have no simple take-home message to offer, no action plan or policy recommendation. Certainly we should not attempt to stop the sort of research offered by the Brain Activity Map. Rather, we should support it, fund it, train our children to carry it forward. The potential benefits, to theoretical knowledge and human well-being, are incredible. But there are costs, or at least risks. It would be best to reach first for a bit of preventive humility, a dash of recognition that there are limits on the self-understanding of even such an expert auto-empiricizer as *homo sapiens*. In Franz Joseph Gall's original phrenological map, the brain area for Circumspection and Forethought was located right next to the brain area for Vanity.

# Notes

1. <http://www.nytimes.com/2013/02/18/science/project-seeks-to-build-map-of-human-brain.html>
2. <http://www.cell.com/neuron/abstract/S0896-6273%2812%2900518-1>

# LANGUAGE, SPEECH, AND FREEDOM

# 41

# COUNTERING ISLAMIC
# EXTREMISM

## Peter Singer

US President Barack Obama hosted a three-day summit on 'Countering Violent Extremism'. That term has already spawned a new abbreviation, CVE, used no fewer than 12 times in a Fact Sheet[1] released by the Obama administration in February 2015.

The Fact Sheet also uses the term 'violent extremism' 31 times. How many times do terms like 'Islam', 'Islamic', or 'Muslim' appear? Zero. There is not even a reference to the Islamic State. That entity is referred to only by the initials, ISIL.

This is not an accident; it is part of a strategy to win the support of mainstream Muslims. Riham Osman, speaking on behalf of the Muslim Public Affairs Council, which participated in the summit, said that using terms like 'radical Islam' harms the cause of stopping the violence.[2] This may partly reflect the Muslim community's understandable fears that associating Islam with terrorism and violence would contribute to an increase in attacks on, or discrimination against, all Muslims.

Another reason that has been offered for not referring to Islamic radicalism or the Islamic State is that to do so concedes the terrorists' claims that they are acting in accordance with Islam's teachings. That might draw others, who regard themselves as pious Muslims, to join them.

Finally, the repeated use of 'Islamic' as part of the description of enemy groups may make it appear that the West is 'at war with Islam'. That could lead more moderate Muslims to fight alongside the extremists, thus broadening the conflict and making it more difficult to end.

Yet there are also problems with seeking to avoid these terms.

The first problem is political. The conservative US Senator Ted Cruz, who was a candidate for the Republican presidential nomination, has said, 'You cannot defeat an opponent if you refuse to acknowledge what it is.' That line could win votes. Indeed, it is never a good idea for a politician to appear to be denying what we can all see before our eyes.

Moreover, because it is obvious to everyone that most of the violent extremism is being carried out in the name of Islam, avoiding the word is unlikely to prevent attacks on Muslims in response to this violence.

A further problem becomes apparent as soon as we ask why it is important that mainstream Muslim leaders stand up in public and say that their religion opposes killing innocent people, or that those who die when committing such acts are not 'martyrs' and will not be rewarded in the afterlife. Why should Muslim leaders, in particular, make such statements, rather than Christian, Buddhist, Jewish, or Hindu leaders?

The answer, once again, is obvious. But it is obvious only because we already know that groups like Al Qaeda, the Islamic State, and the Taliban are not obeying the precepts of Christianity, Buddhism, Judaism, or Hinduism.

At the Washington summit, Obama said that 'all of us have a responsibility to refute the notion that groups like ISIL somehow represent Islam, because that is a falsehood that embraces the terrorist narrative.' At least this statement, unlike the White House Fact Sheet, acknowledges that groups like the Islamic State *claim* to be Islamic. Otherwise, what would be the relevance of this statement to 'countering violent extremism'?

Nonetheless, Obama's assertion that 'all of us' have this responsibility needs to be more narrowly directed. If I tried to get into a debate with any moderately well-educated Islamic State supporter about whether that organization is true to the teachings of Islam, I would lose the argument. I am not sufficiently expert in the Islamic tradition to be confident that extremists are misinterpreting it, and few of us are. The responsibility to which Obama was referring rests with those who are much more learned in Islam than 'all of us'.

Even for people who are learned in Islam, discharging the responsibility Obama has placed on them will not be easy, as a reading of Graeme Wood's revealing account[3] demonstrates. Wood presents a picture of people driven by a firm belief in Islam and knowledgeable about its key texts. Anyone familiar with Christian fundamentalism in the US should be able to discern a pattern in the attitudes taken by religious fundamentalists, independently of the religion to which they adhere.

The Islamic State's spokesmen insist on following the original precepts laid down by the Prophet Mohammed and his earliest followers, understood literally and with no adjustment for different circumstances. Like Christian fundamentalists, they see themselves as preparing for—and helping to bring about—the apocalypse.

Let me emphasize that I am not saying that the beliefs of today's Christian fundamentalists are *morally* on a par with those of today's Muslim fundamentalists. There is a vast moral difference between those who oppose the taking of innocent human life and those who kill people because of their nationality, or what they say, or because they are 'apostates'. But the fundamentalists' worldviews are similar in important respects, regardless of the religion to which they adhere.

By now, the problem with trying to counter those who seek new recruits for 'violent extremism' without focusing on this extremism's Islamic basis should be clear. Those considering joining an extremist Islamic group should be told:

> You believe every other religion to be false, but adherents of many other religions believe just as firmly that your faith is false. You cannot really know who is right, and you could all be wrong. Either way, you do not have a sufficiently well-grounded justification for killing people, or for sacrificing your own life.

Granted, some people are not open to reasoning of any kind, and so will not be swayed by such an argument. But others may be. Why rule it out in advance by denying that much extremist violence is religiously motivated?

# Notes

1. <https://www.whitehouse.gov/the-press-office/2015/02/18/fact-sheet-white-house-summit-countering-violent-extremism>
2. <http://www.bloomberg.com/news/articles/2015-02-18/obama-tries-to-split-religion-from-terrorism-at-summit>
3. <http://www.theatlantic.com/magazine/archive/2015/03/what-isis-really-wants/384980/>

# 42

# DISABLING LANGUAGE

## Neil Levy

The words we use matter. Though maybe they don't 'break our bones' like sticks and stones, words nevertheless can harm us. People certainly feel very strongly about some words and that—by itself—is some reason to avoid using them. It's a defeasible reason (that is, a reason that can be defeated by other considerations) to be sure. The fact that you are offended by what I say doesn't give you a veto over what I say. Nevertheless, it's a consideration that I should attend to.

More seriously, words probably perpetuate disadvantage. For instance, it is likely that implicit biases (unconscious negative attitudes) towards women and minorities play a role in their continuing disadvantage, relative to white men (in Western societies), and the tolerance of belittling or infantilizing language towards members of these groups may reinforce these implicit biases. Words matter because they convey attitudes and indirectly have effects on those who are the target of these attitudes. Research in psychology backs up the contention that the existence of—independently of belief in—stereotypes has real world effects, both on the behaviour of those who are stereotyped and on others too. Those who are stereotyped may suffer stereotype threat, where their performance on tasks suffers because the task is stereotype atypical. For example, women performing tests that are described as diagnostic of mathematical ability perform worse if gender is made salient prior to taking the test.[1] Further, other people may judge and act in ways consistent with the stereotype even when they don't accept it: for instance, people who explicitly reject the notion that black men are more likely to be violent than white nevertheless may be more likely to shoot at a black target holding an ambiguous object than at a white target.[2]

These considerations are very familiar. Most of us have abandoned the use of certain kinds of language, which convey contempt or disrespect towards women and minorities, or which occlude their very existence. For instance, the use of 'mankind' for 'humanity' now strikes most of us as archaic, and we avoid the use of terms like 'girls' for women. What is most contentious in this arena isn't whether we ought to be careful with our language; rather, the issue concerns how far we should go. Almost everyone agrees that we should avoid overtly offensive language ('coons', say, for black people). But some people urge that we think very carefully about the connotations of our language to ensure that we expunge any trace of condescension or insult. However, I believe there is a potential cost in too extensive a policing of language.

These thoughts have been triggered by the recent campaign within academic philosophy to highlight and increase sensitivity to the use of 'ableist' language. Ableist language stands to disability as sexist language stands to gender. Just as we now avoid certain kinds of language because it suggests—and may inadvertently reinforce—the inferiority of women, so we ought to avoid certain kinds of language because it demeans the disabled.

Again, many agree that they ought to avoid overtly offensive language ('crips', 'retards'). But some activists urge us to go much further. There has been a recent campaign to highlight the allegedly ableist connotations of the phrase 'blind review'. 'Blind review' is ableist, it is suggested, because it associates blindness with lack of knowledge and implies that blind people cannot be knowers. Professor Shelley Tremain, who has been at the forefront of a really admirable campaign for increased recognition and accommodation of disabled philosophers, suggests that we replace 'blind review' with 'anonymous review'.[3] I must confess my first response was to regard the whole thing as silly. But I had second thoughts. I no longer think it is silly.

Here's one reason to be suspicious of my initial reaction: when women (and a few men) began to question the unthinking use of sexist language, lots of well-meaning people reacted by thinking that the notion was silly. The people I have in mind may not have been sexist in their explicit commitments. Some of them were well-intentioned. They thought that we should save our energies for fighting for equal rights, and that the movement brought feminism into ridicule. But they overlooked the ways that words can harm. Gradually, people became sensitized to the use of sexist language and we now avoid it. I remain unconvinced that the phrase 'blind review' is problematic (for one thing, it is associated with virtue here, impartiality, rather than with a deficit). Still, it seems easy and costless to avoid the phrase. Given that fact, it seems as though we ought to avoid it.

But there may be hidden costs lurking; not to avoiding the phrase *per se*, but, instead, costs that attach to steps that are required to bring it about that people avoid the phrase. The campaign to replace 'blind review' with 'anonymous review' explicitly seeks to sensitize us to potentially ableist language. Such sensitization may be costly in unanticipated ways.

I doubt that the ableist connotations (if any) of 'blind review' are sufficiently 'live' to play a role in reinforcing the subordination of blind people. What I mean by 'live', in this context, can be brought out by thinking about metaphors. Some metaphors are dead: ordinary speakers are not aware of the fact that they are metaphors at all, and (*a fortiori*) unaware that they imply a resemblance between what is denoted and something else. Consider the word 'sinister', which derives from the Latin for 'left-handed'. It seems to me so dead that there is not the remotest chance that it is harmful to left-handed people. On the other hand, 'gay'—used as a term of disparagement, as in 'that song is so gay'—is alive enough, so that it is plausible that its use is harmful. 'Blind review', it seems to me, is closer to the dead end of the spectrum. The campaign seeks to revivify it as a metaphor; that's what sensitization does. The problem with sensitization is that it makes metaphors live and may lead to some of the very harms it aims to avoid.

Here's an example of what I mean. There have been several recent controversies in the US over the word 'niggardly'.[4] 'Niggardly' is a synonym for 'stingy'. It is etymologically unrelated to the word 'nigger'. However, a number of people have taken offence at the word, because they took them to be related. As a result of these controversies, the following situation has arisen: 'niggardly' is, considered in itself, a perfectly harmless word, but because of the association that has arisen, it is a word that is now best avoided. The Wikipedia entry, on the controversies surrounding the use, notes that people now sometimes use it to have a dig at others: they ask black people not to be niggardly, for instance (thus allowing themselves to be offensive while establishing a bit of plausible deniability). 'Niggardly' may be etymologically unrelated to 'nigger', but it is now guilty by association.

Once you are sensitized to possible associations and suggestions, it is difficult to stop hearing them. Double entendres are a classic example: make one inadvertently in a classroom and from then on every student will hear one in every sentence you say. John Derbyshire (a right-wing journalist whose remarks on race usually tend more to the inflammatory than to the illuminating) notes how the 'niggardly' controversy might cause further words to be become suspect: he gives the example of 'snigger'.

It should be noted that the cost I have highlighted is a cost of sensitizing people to metaphors and thereby revivifying them. There are alternative ways of changing language. For instance, if enough people, in the right kinds of positions (say editors of academic journals) begin using the phrase 'anonymous review', then general usage will shift, without anyone needing to think of why the language is changing. Of course, disability activists may not occupy a sufficient number of sufficiently influential positions to change the language just by changing their own usage. They face a Catch-22: appeal to reasons and thereby risk the costs I've highlighted, or give up on the project altogether.

Saying that there is a cost involved in revivifying metaphors does not entail that this is not something we should do. Perhaps this is a cost worth paying. As is usually the case in applied ethics, highlighting potential pitfalls doesn't end the debate: ethics is messy and complex. It is simply a factor that we need to take into account as we ponder how best to decrease undeserved disadvantage.

# Notes

1. Shapiro, J.R. and Williams, A.M. (2012). 'The role of stereotype threats in undermining girls' and women's performance and interest in STEM fields', *Sex Roles* 66/3: 175–83.
2. Payne, B.K. (2005). 'Conceptualizing control in social cognition: how executive functioning modulates the expression of automatic stereotyping', *Journal of Personality and Social Psychology* 89/4: 488–503.
3. Tremain, S. (2011). 'Ableist language and philosophical associations', *New App.* <http://www.newappsblog.com/2011/07/ableist-language-and-philosophical-associations.html>
4. Wikipedia (n.d.) 'Controversies about the word "niggardly"' <http://en.wikipedia.org/wiki/Controversies_about_the_word_%22niggardly%22>

# 43

# STOP ORIENTALISM?

Kei Hiruta

Over the summer, a weekly event called 'Kimono Wednesdays' at the Museum of Fine Arts (MFA), Boston, provoked controversy. The event was meant to be enjoyable; it encouraged visitors to 'interact' with Claude Monet's *La Japonaise* by trying on a replica of the kimono that the artist's French wife wears in the painting. But it enraged a group of people, who accused the MFA of 'Orientalism'—of reproducing the stereotyped misrepresentation of the East and its people, and perpetuating the domineering attitude towards them. The West once systematically misrepresented the East as barbaric, and colonized it, ostensibly to end barbarism; Kimono Wednesdays, so the allegation went, continued this shameful tradition and reinforced 'stereotypes that justify imperialist domination and enslavement'.[1] The museum did not accept the protestors' demand for a complete closure of the event, but it issued a statement to apologize for the unintended offence and to announce that visitors would henceforth be unable to put on the replicated kimono. The outcry provoked a considerable backlash, yielding impassioned mutual accusations between protestors and counter-protestors.

Curiously, both sides—those asserting 'This is Orientalist!', and those insisting 'No, it's *not* Orientalist!'—share one presumption: the fact that Kimono Wednesdays may reasonably be characterized as Orientalist is by itself sufficient to establish the wrongness of the event. I believe that this presumption is untenable.

Let me begin with an uncontroversial observation. In Japan today, we wear kimono only on special occasions such as weddings and seijin-shiki (celebrating the twentieth year of birth). We wear lighter traditional clothes, for example, yukata, more frequently; but we do so, again, on special occasions such as an evening out for a summer festival.

In our daily lives we wear something less exciting, depending on our preferences and income levels: Prada, Coach, and Uniqlo. An average businessperson in Japan may have the opportunity to wear kimono every decade or two, but he or she wears a suit from Monday to Friday. If culture is a sum of the lived experiences of its participants,[2] wearing kimono is no longer a part of our culture; not, at any rate, as much as Coach and Uniqlo are.

Yukio Mishima, best known for his novel, *The Temple of the Golden Pavilion*, was one of the most perceptive writers to comment on this issue. In his column 'On Clothing', published in 1969, he observed that there was something superficial and inauthentic to the kimono revival occurring in the country in the 1960s. He wrote: 'recently...kimono seems to be adopted in terms of a new fashion, in terms of a renewed interest in something exotic. It is not a part of the rooted, ancient custom that it once was...Women no longer remember as part of their general education how to wear kimono by themselves...Men, too, have lost their natural, customary familiarity with kimono; they now wear it pretentiously, as it were, as a gesture to resist or surpass the convention of the age.'[3]

Mishima's insight deserves the attention of those commenting on Kimono Wednesdays. On his account, which I share, even in the Japan of the late 1960s, kimono could not be worn without a dose of what we today call Orientalist fantasy. If those taking selfies in front of Monet's *La Japonaise* in Boston in 2015 are Orientalists, so were the Japanese men and women who joined the kimono revival in Tokyo in 1969. The difference is one of degree, not kind. And the degree is not great, either, because both groups of people are moderns, who cannot claim an unbroken cultural lineage from the past. One could, of course, argue that modernity itself was imposed on Japan by Western imperialists beginning with the nineteenth-century navy commodore, Matthew C. Perry and his proto-neo-liberal gunships. This ostensibly anti-imperialist view, however, disguises a historically inaccurate and morally condescending paternalism, implying that modernization took place in Japan without an exercise of collective agency. The truth is that the nation has embraced modernity, albeit under varying degrees of external pressure. If we no longer remember how to wear kimono, it is in no small measure due to the decisions that the Japanese themselves have made, at least since 1868.

The decline of the habit of kimono dressing, as Mishima also noted, was not and could not be a stand-alone loss. It entailed a loss of other, organically connected cultural ingredients, including the traditional class division and sexual hierarchy. In this respect, the disappearance of kimono dressers from the streets of Tokyo, Osaka, etc. is comparable to the disappearance of non-human creatures from modernized areas of the country. As significant decrease in the population of butterflies indicates a loss of their entire habitat, the disappearance of kimono dressers indicates a loss of the old Japan and its way of life that inspired nineteenth-century *Japonisme.*

As is well known, Mishima himself considered the modern Japanese society in which he found himself absurd, ugly, and even grotesque, and half-seriously fancied a return to a pre-Meiji world of yesterday. Yet, he had the candidacy to acknowledge the moral gain accompanying the aesthetic loss; though the artist, always willing to subordinate non-aesthetic values to aesthetic ones, denied that the former outweighed the latter. 'I think the time when women were always crying was wonderful!' he said, in his characteristically dark, mocking, and aphoristic tone. Those of us who do not share his aestheticism are entitled to weigh moral and aesthetic values differently. We ought to be glad that we no longer live in a time when women in exquisitely beautiful kimono 'were quietly weeping, always, somewhere in the house'.[4] Perhaps, we should be glad that kimono can no longer be worn *anywhere* without a dose of Orientalist fantasy. Perhaps.

It is a curious fact about our contemporary culture that, in places like Boston at least, the wrongness of Orientalism is considered so self-evident that those commenting on Kimono Wednesdays have largely focused on *whether* the event is Orientalist, sidestepping harder questions as to specifically what is wrong with Orientalism and whether the wrongness of Orientalism should override other considerations. But the latter set of questions demands greater attention not least because, as I have argued, the pervasiveness of Orientalism today might be inseparable from the moral progress we have made in the past couple of centuries. Addressing the relevant issues fully is a challenging task; for starters, we should recognize the *triviality* of the oft-made assertions about the MFA event: 'This is Orientalist!', 'No, it's *not* Orientalist!'

# Notes

1. Decolonize Our Museums, (29 July 2015). 'Full response to MFA "Kimono Wednesdays" + "Flirting with the exotic"'. <http://decolonizeourmuseums. tumblr.com/post/125348836324/full-response-to-mfa-kimono-wednesdays>

2. Raymond Williams is the most influential advocate of this conception of culture. See, for example, his (1958). *Culture and Society: 1780–1950* (London: Chatto & Windus).

3. Yukio Mishima ([1969] 1976). 'Fukusō ni tsuite' *Mishima Yukio zenshū* ['On clothing', in *Collected Works of Yukio Mishima*] (Tokyo: Shinchō-sha), 33: 338–39. My translation.

4. Yukio Mishima (1976). 'Poppukōn no shinrei-jutsu: Yokoo Tadanori-ron' [posthumous publication], *Mishima Yukio zenshū* ['Popcorn spiritualism: on Tadanori Yokoo', *Collected Works of Yukio Mishima*] (Tokyo: Shinchō-sha), 35: 228. My translation.

# 44

# THE NAKED TRUTH

Roger Crisp

Stephen Gough, over a series of sentences, has served nearly six years in custody in the UK for refusing to wear clothes in public.[1] A former lorry driver and marine, Gough shows no sign of changing his view on the importance of nudity, and it is conceivable that he will spend most of the rest of his life behind bars. Why does he do it? It's not entirely clear, but his position appears to be grounded on the value of living an autonomous life: 'We can either end up living a life that others expect of us or live based on our own truth. The difference is the difference between living a conscious life or one that is unconscious. And that's the difference between living and not living.'

On the face of it, Gough's decision sounds like a paradigmatic example of the kind of 'experiments in living' that John Stuart Mill, in his book, *On Liberty*,[2] thought no one should be prevented from attempting, except in so far as they harm others: 'the worth of different modes of life should be proved practically, when anyone thinks fit to try them.' But in fact Mill himself would probably have advocated Gough's imprisonment on grounds of indecency: '[T]here are many acts which, being directly injurious only to the agents themselves, ought not to be legally interdicted, but which, if done publicly, are a violation of good manners, and coming thus within the category of offences against others, may rightly be prohibited. Of this kind are offences against decency.'

The tension here arises within Mill's utilitarianism itself. On the one hand, he recognizes the importance to human happiness of our following our own paths in life. On the other, he sees that our so doing can often seriously upset or threaten others, sometimes to the point where the best outcome may involve the restriction of individual freedom.

But, if that were Mill's view on the Gough case, would his siding with convention here be a mere product of Victorian stuffiness? Yes, people may get upset, perhaps repulsed, perhaps even quite frightened, by seeing a man wandering around without clothes. But maybe it would be more valuable, in the longer term, for us to allow experiments in living that upset others: we may discover more valuable ways of life and, even if we don't, our failures will provide a contrast against which truly happiness-promoting modes of existence can stand out. What, really, is the utilitarian value in having taboos concerning public nudity?

I can see the force of this liberal, pro-Gough argument. It is not difficult to imagine a world in which nakedness is universally accepted, and it may well be that such a world would be happier without our hang-ups about clothes. But a central issue here is feasibility. Even if Gough's experiment catches on, the upshot is likely to be a large increase in genuine offence and alarm, as well as an increase in sexually motivated exhibitionism, universal acceptance of which is even less likely in the longer term. In a sense, Gough is harmless: there is a possible world in which what he does harms no one. But in this world he does cause harm. And of course the chances of Gough's changing attitudes and then the law are minuscule, especially in a country such as the UK, where the cool atmospheric climate is matched with a prudish social one. My advice to Gough on release would be either to live in a naturist colony, or to find some less alarming way of expressing himself among the rest of us.

But what about people who are offended by, say, the wearing of burqas? And what if this feeling of offence becomes really quite widespread? Does Mill have to allow that the wearing of the burqa can 'rightly be prohibited'? Well, he can't just ignore the unpleasantness for those who are offended (an implication of his utilitarianism which many would itself find offensive). But he would of course be fully aware that such feelings of offence are part of an overall harmful attitude towards others which not only shouldn't be legitimized, but should be actively discouraged. People who wear burqas should be allowed to go about their business undisturbed; people who wear nothing should not.

## Notes

1. <http://www.guardian.co.uk/lifeandstyle/2012/mar/23/naked-rambler-prison>
2. Mill, J.S. (1869). *On Liberty* (London: Longman, Roberts & Green), ch. 4, para. 9.

# 45

# PORN, CONDOMS, AND LIBERTY

## Kyle T. Edwards

On 6 November 2012 the citizens of Los Angeles County confronted an unusually explicit question at the voting box: should porn performers be required to wear condoms while filming? Nearly 56% said yes.

The primary backer of this measure—Measure B—was the AIDS Healthcare Foundation. It argued that Measure B was important for protecting both performer and public health from the spread of HIV, particularly in protecting performers from workplace hazards.

Considering that one of the biggest porn studios experienced a 30% drop in sales when it tried filming with condoms, the adult film industry is unsurprisingly Measure B's greatest opponent. It claims that the measure is expensive to enforce and unnecessary, since the industry already has effective STI testing procedures in place.

Most people agree that the state must provide strong reasons for interfering in adults' decisions when these choices do not result in harm to third parties. To justify the condom requirement, then, proponents must show either 1) that the choice not to wear condoms actually does harm third parties, 2) that performers don't choose but are rather forced into condom-less sex, or 3) that choice in the porn industry should be restricted by standard workplace safety regulations.

## Basis 1: Harm to third parties

Proponents of Measure B claim that the failure of porn performers to wear condoms may harm third parties by threatening public health. This argument seems to rest on the empirical claim that porn performers are a greater 'cause' of STI prevalence in the general population than the average citizen. Otherwise, this type of public health argument would suggest that we enforce condom use upon all citizens. Importantly, then, proponents need to show not only that the rates of STIs are higher in the population of porn performers, but also that they substantially impact the sexual health of the general population.

Before filming commences, an industry database is used to confirm that all performers have tested negative for HIV, syphilis, chlamydia, and gonorrhea in the past 14 days.[1] The industry has detailed plans in place in the event of a positive HIV test result: studios across the country are notified and required to cease filming, sometimes for months at a time, until potentially infected actors are tested. Such procedures appear to work surprisingly well: there has been only one reported case of HIV transmission on a porn set in the US in the past 11 years.[2] For perspective, over 47,000 individuals were diagnosed with HIV in the US in 2013 alone.[3] Studies do show that porn performers test positive for chlamydia and gonorrhea more frequently than the general public,[4] but it remains to be shown that this substantially impacts individuals outside of the industry; both are treatable when diagnosed and the 14-day testing cycle ensures rapid diagnosis.

The second harm-to-third-parties argument posits that teenagers watching porn will conclude that 'hot sex is sex without a condom',[5] fail to use condoms, and thus be at higher risk for contracting STIs. This may be true. But the argument that we should therefore infringe upon the liberty of performers gets things the wrong way around. State intervention should focus on altering the choices of teenagers through comprehensive sexual health education, not those of porn performers.

It would be easier for the state to achieve many desirable ends, such as crime reduction, if we didn't have such strong protections on liberties, such as those to prevent unreasonable search and seizure. We think rightly, however, that protecting these liberties is worth some additional cost and inconvenience in reaching that end. Even if it would be easier to increase condom use amongst teenagers by banning performers from filming without condoms, the presumption in favour of liberty suggests that the state must accept somewhat more onerous means to achieving its ends.

## Basis 2: Porn performers are not free to choose—they either wear condoms or lose their jobs

The condom mandate might be justified if porn performers are, in a morally significant sense, 'forced' to have unprotected sex or are otherwise significantly non-autonomous in their decision-making. We generally find it permissible for the state to intervene if an individual is being forced to do something that endangers her health or well-being. Although the question of when one is forced to do something is contested, it seems a good enough formulation for our purposes that a person is forced to do something when she has no reasonable or acceptable alternatives.

But the claim that porn performers in Los Angeles County have no reasonable or acceptable alternatives is highly doubtful. Even if there were no producers willing to film with condoms—and, as it happens, there are a few—there are a range of unskilled jobs (assuming the worst case scenario in which a porn performer has no other talents or education) in Los Angeles that provide reasonable and acceptable alternatives if performers were unwilling to take the risk of condom-less sex. Performers hail from diverse career backgrounds, from models, actors, and strippers to teachers, writers, and administrative assistants. The construction of an image in which a pitiful porn performer is forced to have unsafe sex is misguided and sets a dangerously broad precedent for what counts as force.

## Basis 3: Condoms can be mandated as a standard occupational health and safety measure, like requiring hardhats for construction workers

The president of the AIDS Healthcare Foundation has compared Measure B's spot inspections to ensure condom use to hot-dog-stand health inspections. Other proponents of Measure B assert that it simply extends state regulations requiring protective equipment for occupational exposure to blood and other potentially infectious materials, originally crafted for doctors, lab technicians, and dentists, to the adult film industry.

True, the porn set is a workplace. But we don't, in fact, treat all workplaces the same. We allow vastly different levels of risk in the workplace based largely on the understanding that a competent adult should be able to assume a greater risk of harm in his career if he is fully aware of that risk. Racecar drivers accept a much greater risk of harm in their workplace than schoolteachers and accountants, and arguably more than porn performers. Yet most people would likely balk if a 100 mph speed limit were imposed on NASCAR races.

Furthermore, the cost to a lab technician of wearing protective gear is minimal in terms of time and inconvenience, and does not seriously undermine her job. However, a person can reasonably argue that sex with a condom is significantly different from sex without a condom, both in terms of expression and inconvenience. Adult film actor James Deen argues that filming without a condom allows him to portray a particular fantasy,[6] while Nina Hartley explains that the nature of porn sex—far longer and with many more stops and starts than sex for the average person—makes the use of condoms painful and can cause vaginal tearing.[7]

None of these three arguments provides a strong enough basis for the serious infringement on performers' liberties that is entailed by government-enforced condom use.

## Notes

1. Free Speech Coalition (8 December 2013). 'An FAQ about STIs, testing and moratoriums'. <http://freespeechcoalition.com/an-faq-about-stis-testing-and-moratoriums/>

2. Romero, Dennis (30 December 2014). 'Porn star transmits HIV on-set, California officials say', *LA Weekly*. <http://www.laweekly.com/news/porn-star-transmits-hiv-on-set-california-officials-say-5314217>

3. Centers for Disease Control and Prevention (12 March 2015). 'HIV in the United States: at a glance'. <http://www.cdc.gov/hiv/statistics/basics/ataglance.html>

4. Grudzen, C.R. and Kemdt, P.R. (2007). 'The adult film industry: time to regulate?' *PLoS Medicine* 4. <http://journals.plos.org/plosmedicine/article?id=10.1371/journal.pmed.0040126#pmed-0040126-b007>

5. Dines, G. (12 November 2012). 'LA County's Measure B is a major win for safe sex in adult entertainment,' *The Guardian*. <http://www.theguardian.com/commentisfree/2012/nov/12/la-county-measureb-safe-sex>

6. *ABC News* (9 November 2012). 'Porn industry against Measure B, mandatory condom measure passed in Los Angeles County where adult films made. <http://abcnews.go.com/Health/porn-industry-measure-mandatory-condom-measure-passed-los/story?id=17673377&singlePage=true> last accessed 6 April 2015.

7. Hess, A. (25 October 2012). 'Porn stars may soon have to wear condoms. Will you still watch?' *Slate*. <http://www.slate.com/blogs/xx_factor/2012/10/25/california_s_measure_b_what_s_so_bad_about_condoms_in_porn.html> last accessed 6 April 2015.

# 46

# SHOULD MEN BE ALLOWED TO DISCUSS ABORTION?

Jim A.C. Everett

Oxford University student feminists have been kicking up a storm. The 'pro-life' group Oxford Students for Life (OSFL) organized a debate on abortion which inspired some troubling attacks.[1] The official Oxford student feminist group (WomCam) is rather intolerant of any pro-life rhetoric, but what really irked them this time was that the debate was between two men. WomCam issued a statement:

> It is absurd to think we should be listening to two cisgender men debate about what people with uteruses should be doing with their bodies. By only giving a platform to these men, OSFL are participating in a culture where reproductive rights are limited and policed by people who will never experience needing an abortion.

In the end the event was banned, sparking national coverage and commentary about free speech in British universities.

Note that the OSFL group had already hosted two all-women panel debates on abortion in the same year, so the criticism wasn't that they only have men speak in their debates generally. It was that on this particular occasion men were speaking. One of the organizers repeated in an opinion piece for *The Independent*:[2]

> [OSFL] thought it was appropriate to let men discuss if and when women should be able to make fundamental decisions about their own bodies. Neither will ever have to consider having an abortion. As you can imagine, those of us with uteruses were incredibly angry that they were able to speak for and over us.

The implication is that (biological) men should not be able to discuss abortion in public settings because they are men and could not themselves have an abortion.

So are there any good reasons to think that only women should be allowed to discuss abortion?

Embedded within the worrying debate is the reasonable claim that, when deliberating over complex social and political issues, we should take care to listen to the views of those members of society most affected. Discussion on abortion certainly requires the input of women, since the issue has such a big impact on many of their lives. It is vital that an effort is made to consider their experiences as it bears on this debate. Yet it doesn't follow that *only* women should be allowed to discuss abortion in public contexts (debates, speeches, articles).

First, abortion is not an issue that only affects women. Abortion causes the death of both male and female foetuses. And how could we possibly think that a woman aborting her male partner's foetus against his wishes would have no bearing on him?

But, second, even if we accepted the flawed notion that only (biological) women are affected by abortion, the principle that, therefore, only women can discuss it patently fails, leading to farcical conclusions. The logic that one must have personally experienced, or have the potential to experience, an issue in order to argue about it would imply that, in the abortion debate, the views of the infertile, transgendered, or post-menopausal childless should be excluded.

That's not a conclusion most of us could endorse. We don't think that only homosexuals can discuss gay rights, only black people can argue about affirmative action, and only disabled people can debate equal rights in the workplace. Indeed, had, historically, these restrictions been imposed, it is extremely unlikely that any progress on these basic moral issues would ever have occurred.

If we insisted that people are only entitled to discuss things that are personally relevant to them, we would soon have to conclude that no-one could ever discuss anything. 'Sorry, you can't talk about disability support because you don't have a disability'; 'Oh, you do? Well it's not a mental health disability, so you still can't'; 'Oh, it is? Well, it's not a bipolar disorder, so you still can't discuss it'; 'Oh, it is? Well, you still can't enter the conversation because I'm also homosexual as well as bipolar, and you couldn't possibly understand the delicate interplay of these two characteristics.' And so on, *ad infinitum,* into the arms of nonsense.

And what are the implications of this mindset for practical ethics? Should all men in philosophy departments stop their work on topics like abortion? Should anyone without addiction problems eschew research on addiction and moral responsibility? Should anyone who doesn't live in the developing world shun investigations into charity and aid? Should anyone who isn't a non-human animal discontinue their analysis of animal rights?

Any attempt to restrict debate of particular subjects to certain groups inevitably results in daft inconsistencies. Everyone has a legitimate right to participate in discussion so long as they belong to just one group: the human group.

## Notes

1. <http://oxfordstudent.com/2014/11/17/abortion-culture-debate-provokes-student-outrage/>
2. <http://www.independent.co.uk/voices/comment/i-helped-shut-down-an-abortion-debate-between-two-men-because-my-uterus-isnt-up-for-their-discussion-9867200.html>

# EVIL, DISGUST, SHAME, RUDENESS, AND JOY

# 47

# A REFLECTION ON CONFRONTING EVIL

## Regina Rini

The New York state legislature has approved a bill endorsing same-sex marriage,[1] bringing the state in line with such bastions of extravagant liberalism as Argentina, Nepal, and Iowa. Taking to the airwaves before the vote, New York Archbishop Timothy Dolan declared[2] the legislation an 'ominous threat'. Same-sex marriage is 'detrimental for the common good,' said the Archbishop; it violates 'the natural law that's embedded in every man and woman'.

This entry is not *about* gay marriage; I will not present an argument for the moral necessity of marriage equality. Similarly, I will not write about the moral necessity of racial integration in public education, or the moral necessity of women's suffrage. Merely raising such issues for argument implies an open question about the human dignity of the people affected. My *starting point* is that marriage equality is such an issue. My question, instead, is this: how are we to deal with those responsible for our collective failure to decisively conclude this argument, the existence of which is morally repugnant?

It is important that Archbishop Dolan himself wields normative vocabulary. Legal recognition of same-sex marriage is 'unjust and immoral'. The conjunction is infuriatingly instructive. Not only is it 'unjust' to ensure equal treatment before the law to a marginalized minority. It is also 'immoral' to extend affirming social sanction to the effort of two vulnerable mortals to create durable meaning in the solemnified commitment of their love and devotion to one another.

When I read that an adult has said such things publicly, especially in the course of trying to influence policy, I intuitively conclude that this person lacks elementary moral sensitivity. I cannot avoid thinking that such disrespect, directed towards some of the most centrally human aspirations of fellow citizens, betrays in the speaker a gapingly deficient character. Archbishop Dolan seemingly marks himself a sad figure, whose behaviour would be worthy of only pity, were it not aggressively directed at the lives of innocent others.

But my reaction is a mistake. Yes, as a matter of practical politics, Archbishop Dolan must be resisted. So long as he busily dispatches underlings to Albany, or anywhere else progress might be transpiring, we should attempt to neutralize his influence. Yet this political aim doesn't require adopting the attitude I described a moment ago, that simmering fusion of contempt and pity. Our political aim is compatible with a reflective rejection of that attitude; we might resist Archbishop Dolan's abominable ends without adopting a dismissive stance towards his person. Indeed, I think this is what we ought to do: our (or, anyway, my) intuitive vilification of people like Archbishop Dolan cannot withstand reflective scrutiny.

I assume here that Archbishop Dolan's assertions about morality are sincere, that he truly does believe marriage equality to be morally wrong and unjust. He would, I assume, ground these views in respect for the millennia of Christian ethical tradition, drawing ultimately from an intensely selective sort of Bible interpretation. These are terrible arguments, but they show a fallible intellect, rather than a flawed character, and we are not justified in morally condemning someone simply for being unequipped to escape a deep cognitive hole.

Perhaps—it is tempting to claim—people like the Archbishop are self-deceived, and culpably so. Their apparent arguments, so many finely sharpened apologia and delicately brushed distinctions, are only unconscious techniques for keeping from view an outrageously bigoted heart. It is not insincerity, as the deception is not deliberate; it is instead a failure of custodianship for one's own mind. If this is the true nature of Archbishop Dolan, then we might feel justified in condemning him, if only to issue a call to responsibility for the consequences of negligently unleashing one's own disordered demons in the public square.

Maybe. But that is speculative psychodrama. If our ultimate aim is to secure a form of public debate respectful to the moral agency of all, we cannot begin from the condescending assertion that we understand our opponents' minds better than they do. In fact, none of us can fully appreciate the secret mechanisms populating our own internal behind-the-scenes. Accusations of psychological bad faith are universally corrosive, as much a threat to the basic institutions of giving reasons and hearing arguments as to any particular individual.

So we must assume that Archbishop Dolan is sincere, and is not a self-deceived bigot. What, then, is he? Mistaken, yes. But still a person, a moral agent, whose *capacity* for participation in public discourse must be respected, even as in practice it stirs a debate destructive of others' agency. The aim of public morality, of any richer means of living together than mutually grudging accommodation, presupposes a shared commitment to understanding one another as fully constituted, respect-deserving agential equals. Archbishop Dolan's comments, implicitly predicated on the inferiority of homosexuals, are signal failures to uphold this aim. We do not improve matters by engaging in further such failures, now directed at him.

I began by considering two intensely incompatible moral visions: of marriage equality as unjust and immoral, and of that very condemnation of marriage equality as emanating from a stunted moral sensibility. If we wish to see the former viewpoint shuttered, then we should begin by relinquishing the latter. This is a terrifically difficult aspiration, requiring us to keep in sight the evil perpetrated by the public actions of people like Archbishop Dolan, without idly slipping towards an unhelpful dismissal of the erring person. The lesson here is old, and familiar, and good. Hate the sin. But try to love, or at least to respect, the sinner.

## Notes

1. <http://www.reuters.com/article/2011/06/19/us-newyork-gaymarriage-idUSTRE75I2PC20110619>
2. <http://cityroom.blogs.nytimes.com/2011/06/17/archbishop-calls-gay-marriage-bill-an-ominous-threat/>

# 48

# SHAME ABOUT
# THE INTERNET

Andreas Kappes

Engaging in social media runs some risks. An emotional tweet, or a Facebook post after a couple of pints might land you in trouble with friends and family: in extreme instances it could cost you your job and bring worldwide notoriety.

Justine Sacco is probably the most famous case. Before boarding an airplane to South Africa from the US, she tweeted to her small number of Twitter followers (170) what was either a racist comment or, as she would have it, a misfired, ill-calculated joke. 'Going to Africa. Hope I don't get AIDS. Just kidding. I'm white!' When she landed, she was trending at number one worldwide on Twitter, people were openly harassing her, and among many things, wishing her fired from her job; a wish that her company duly granted. Even worse were the emotional consequences of the incident. 'I cried out my body weight in the first 24 hours,' Sacco said. 'It was incredibly traumatic.' The journalist Jon Ronson wrote an article[1] about this case and later a book:[2] *So You've Been Publicly Shamed* portrays people who'd suffered from online harassment. They include Monica Lewinsky, who describes[3] herself as the first victim of online shaming. Lewinsky had severe suicidal tendencies in the aftermath of her affair with President Clinton; her mother made her shower with an open bathroom door out of fear of what she might do.

Why does online harassment have such devastating consequences?

The word 'shame' is at the core of the problem and reappears in terms such as 'online shaming' or 'cyber shaming'. Shame and guilt are the two cardinal moral emotions signifying that we have failed to live up to our own moral standards; both emotions give immediate feedback or 'internal punishment' for our transgressions. People often use shame and guilt as synonyms but decades of research show that they are distinct.[4] While both can be elicited by the same action (for example, tweeting an inappropriate joke or falling in love with your boss), and both can be experienced privately or publicly, they differ in the subject and the concerns involved. The subject of shame is oneself as a person, whereas the subject of guilt is a particular action. Hence, shame evokes self-centred concerns: 'Am I a bad person?' and 'Do others think that I'm a bad person?' Guilt, in contrast, increases interpersonal concerns: 'I hope I didn't hurt the other person.' Online criticism and harassment is strongly linked to shame. Online, people seldom focus on the particular transgression a person committed, but rather immediately target the person. Sacco became a white supremacist and racist, Lewinsky a slut and home-wrecker. This may be partly due to a fundamental attribution error, our tendency to think that other people's behaviour is caused by their character, while attributing our own bad behaviour to challenging circumstances; another person's bad tweet reveals their flawed character, our misguided ones only highlight our stressful life. Armed with the knowledge of another person's 'true' character, we begin attacking it.[5]

While both shame and guilt can be evoked by the same moral transgression, they have different consequences: shame is associated with a host of terrible ones, which more often than not outweigh the severity of the 'crime'. Research shows that in the direct aftermath, feelings of worthlessness and powerlessness induced by shame often lead to attempts to deny, hide, or escape a certain situation.[6] While a sense of guilt instead might lead to constructive and proactive attempts to solve a situation (for example, quickly deleting a post and apologizing for it), people who feel shame are less likely to apologize and more likely to blame something or somebody else. Monica Lewinsky, for instance, denied her relationship with Clinton and tried to persuade a co-worker to lie under oath about it. Even worse, shame also leads to anger, aggression, and the desire to punish and harm other people. Such actions are then interpreted by the attackers as further evidence for why the other person is both wrong and horrible, and a sad, self-reinforcing circle—which can be witnessed daily on the internet—ensues. And since shame is related to the question of whether or not one is a good, valuable person, it should come as no surprise to learn that feelings of shame are related to depression and even suicidal tendencies.

So, what should we do? As participants on the internet, and social media especially, the most important step we can take is to focus any attention on the action itself, rather than making inferences about the underlying character of the responsible party. Saying something stupid, writing something stupid, and doing something stupid are part of the human condition. When we criticize somebody else on the internet, we would be wise to remind ourselves about how little we really know about another person and their situation. And if we ourselves have committed a moral transgression on the internet, we should try to give explanations for this transgression that are within ourselves, yet at the same time temporary and controllable: we were too emotional writing that blog post; we were too exhausted from pressures at work. Such thinking leaves us with responsibility for an action, while allowing us to deal with it in a constructive way.

Guilt offers redemption, shame does not.

# Notes

1. <http://www.nytimes.com/2015/02/15/magazine/how-one-stupid-tweet-ruined-justine-saccos-life.html?_r=1>
2. <http://www.theguardian.com/books/2015/mar/15/publicly-shamed-jon-ronson-is-shame-necessary-jennifer-jacquet-review-think-before-you-tweet>
3. <http://www.ted.com/talks/monica_lewinsky_the_price_of_shame?language=en>
4. See <http://ubc-emotionlab.ca/wp-content/files_mf/tangneytracyselfandidhandbk chapter2012published.pdf> <http://www.ncbi.nlm.nih.gov/pmc/articles/PMC 3083636/pdf/nihms288615.pdf>
5. Ironically, the people who feel the most insecure about a certain character attribute (for example, being honest) are also the ones prone to call out other people on it (see research on self-completion theory: <https://en.wikipedia.org/wiki/Symbolic_self-completion_theory>). Such public criticism is a symbolic act that helps make people feel secure about themselves.
6. See <http://ubc-emotionlab.ca/wp-content/files_mf/tangneytracyselfandid handbkchapter2012published.pdf>

# 49

# IN DEFENCE OF
# DRINKING ALONE

## Hannah Maslen and Rebecca Roache

All *silent* intoxication has something shameful in it; that is, intoxication that does not enliven sociability and the reciprocal communication of thoughts

Immanuel Kant, *Anthropology from a Pragmatic Point of View*

Enjoying several glasses of wine at a dinner party, sharing a case of beers with a friend while watching the football, or toasting an achievement with a round of cocktails are all considered normal and acceptable. Less socially acceptable is to do any of these things in solitude. Even holding the amount of alcohol constant between settings, drinking alone rather than with friends is often seen as more troubling.

We'll explore two reasons for thinking drinking alone is worse than drinking in company. The first involves the inference that drinking alone is symptomatic of an underlying problem with the drinker. The second involves a moral disapproval of drinking alone.

## The view that solo drinking is bad for solo drinkers

One reason to be concerned for the solo drinker is that she strikes us as more at risk of pathological alcohol dependency than the social drinker. In so far as a person's solo drinking *is* associated with addiction, we agree that there is cause for concern. However, in such a case, solo drinking is an indicator of a problem, not the problem itself. The real problem for such a person is her relationship with alcohol *per se*, not that she consumes it alone. One does not address her alcohol dependency by encouraging her to find a drinking partner, but by encouraging her to drink less alcohol.

Another health-related worry is that alcohol is associated with depression. This association holds regardless of whether one drinks alone or in company. However, we might be more likely to suspect depression in a solo drinker because he appears withdrawn, and so fits our view of what depressed people are like better than the social drinker.

Alternatively, we might pity the solo drinker. If only she had a friend, she would be drinking with them. Or perhaps the alcohol is itself a substitute for a friend.

## The view that solo drinkers are bad

These examples illustrate that drinking alone might be thought worse than drinking in company because it may be indicative of a problem. What about drinking alone when it is *not* indicative of a problem? The quotation from Kant, above, encapsulates the view—still common today—that drinking alone is morally problematic. The assumption seems to be that drinking *ought* to be a social activity: the odd beer alone is fine, but any more than this requires the presence of others for moral legitimacy.

It is true that drinking is often a social activity, but we suggest that there is no defensible reason why it *should* be. What is acceptable drinking behaviour in company is equally acceptable in private. Moral disapprobation of solitary drinkers is a product of misconceiving social norms as moral principles.

## Bias in favour of being sociable

There are various reasons why drinking is viewed primarily as a social activity, including the role that it has historically played in our culture. However, it is surprising that drinking to oil the wheels of social intercourse tends not to attract disapprobation, since certain well-known arguments in applied ethics—specifically arguments in the ethics of human enhancement—find a natural analogy here.

For example, a common argument against enhancement in sport ('doping') and cognitive enhancement has it that achievements made with the aid of enhancement are less valuable than those made without enhancement. This is one reason why Olympic medalists who fail drugs tests are stripped of their medals. We might view drinking in social settings as a form of social enhancement: Ernest Hemmingway once said, 'I drink to make other people more interesting', and many of us have deepened a friendship with someone over a beer. Yet people do not view friendships cemented with alcohol as *less valuable* than those that develop solely in sober settings. Another example: the idea of enhancing our romantic attachments through the use of drugs has been met with alarm by some people. Yet nobody is alarmed by familiar ways of using alcohol to enhance our relationships. Bonding with a colleague over a post-work drink or celebrating an achievement with a bottle of champagne between friends is not seen as morally objectionable.

Even so, viewing alcohol as a social enhancement does not do full justice to its value for us. Drinking often involves appreciating—in gastronomic or aesthetic ways—the drink itself, and one can do this alone as well as in company. Indeed, perhaps the tastes and textures of alcoholic drinks are best appreciated when not distracted by friends: wine tasting, after all, can require a great deal of attention and reflection.

We do not suggest that we *ought* to disapprove of social drinking. Rather, we want to highlight that, whatever the reason for social drinking being viewed as morally preferable to solo drinking, it is not because there exist no moral arguments against social drinking. Such arguments do exist, but people do not make use of them. Excepting extreme cases where social drinking is problematic—such as the danger-ous drinking game Neknominate[1]—few of us have the moral intuition that social drinking is objectionable. Why, then, do people disapprove of solo drinking?

One possible explanation is a cultural bias in favour of sociable behaviour and against solitary behaviour. Susan Cain, author of *Quiet: The Power of Introverts In a World That Can't Stop Talking*, argues that there is such a bias. According to Cain, Western society overvalues extroversion and undervalues introversion. Introverts tend to be misunderstood, often being seen as anti-social when in fact they simply need more time alone, and have as much to offer society as do extroverts.

If this bias in favour of extroversion extends to popular views about drinking, this might explain the moral stigma attached to drinking alone. Cain's work illustrates that we often—without good reason—view solitary people as anti-social and shy. The same inclination might be responsible for us viewing solo drinkers with suspicion. To be sure, alcohol causes serious problems for many people. But, among other drinkers, it plays a valuable and morally innocuous role in our social lives. There seems to be no reason why it cannot also play a valuable and morally innocuous role in our solitary lives.

## Note

1. <http://www.bbc.com/news/health-26302180>

# 50

# LADY THATCHER IS DEAD

*Pop open the champagne*

David Edmonds

Margaret Thatcher has died. A few people have declared that this is grounds for celebration. 'A great day,' they have announced. Pop open the champagne. There have even been street parties. An impromptu chorus of 'Maggie Maggie Maggie, dead dead dead' erupted at one such event.[1]

Well, we know that Lady Thatcher was the most divisive British prime minister of the twentieth century. Still, this response puzzles me.

Let's put to one side cases where death is good for the person who dies; perhaps because their life was one of intense suffering. The puzzle is why would a person's death ever be good in any way for *other* people?

There are various possible answers to this.

First, a death might be good, at least in one way, if the person who died was doing great damage or would have done great damage in the future. It would have certainly been good if the target of the 20 July 1944 assassination attempt in Germany had been killed.[2]

Second, it might be good if the death were a useful deterrent in some way to other people. That's one rationale people use to justify capital punishment.

But neither of these arguments applies to Thatcher, an octogenarian with dementia. Those who vehemently oppose everything she stood for—and who believe her economic and social policies were disastrous for Britain and beyond—can't plausibly maintain that her existence in her dotage made it any more likely that her policies would be promoted or implemented. Perhaps, for some, the trauma of the Thatcher years was so great that only with her death can they psychologically heal. This too seems implausible.[3]

A third reason for celebrating death (though not one I would ever give) might be on retributive grounds: if, by dying, a person received their just deserts. But again, it can't be the case that those who declared themselves happy at Thatcher's passing think that the death of a woman who's lived to a ripe old age reflects some sort of natural justice.

All I can imagine is that the celebrators somehow believe that Lady Thatcher's existence in the world was a kind of metaphysical stain on the universe. That's one heck of a thing to believe.

So, if advice in such situations were not counterproductive, I would tell those hostile to Margaret Thatcher to keep the champagne for a future occasion. They need not celebrate her life. Nor should they celebrate her death.

## Notes

1. <http://www.theguardian.com/politics/2013/apr/08/margaret-thatcher-death-party-brixton-glasgow>
2. One of several attempts to assassinate Hitler. <https://www.jewishvirtuallibrary.org/jsource/Holocaust/julyplot.html>
3. Although, this would be less implausible for very extreme cases. For victims of, say, a genocide. For them, I can imagine that hearing of the death of the orchestrator of the genocide would provide a kind of release, even if the person who died no longer posed any threat.

# 51

# STEAMY CALAMARI AND TRANS-SPECIES EROTICISM

Anders Sandberg

Imagine a naked, beautiful person of your preferred gender. Now imagine that they sensuously fondle a sausage. They gently caress it, they lick it, they eventually insert it somewhere...

While no doubt some of my readers have been turned off at this point, I think few would argue that depicting this scene is significantly more immoral than depicting the scene sans sausage. While one might have various concerns with pornography, self-stimulation, or the waste of food, most modern people would regard the scene as harmless 'food play'. In fact, sexual and erotic uses of food are widespread and, at least in their milder forms, regarded as pretty tame fetishes.

What about pictures of playing around with calamari? Well, at least the UK legal system appears to find them objectionable. A man was accused of possessing extreme porn images, including images of humans and animals having sex, and the news media focused on a particular image involving a dead cephalopod[1] (it is not entirely certain whether it was a squid or an octopus). Leaving aside the legal issue of what constitutes obscenity, what about the *ethical* issue? Is there really anything wrong with having sex with a dead cephalopod? Or having pictures of the act?

The most common moral arguments against zoophilia are that it is disgusting (invoking the wisdom of repugnance) and against the natural order. But the former—disgust—is culturally variable, and the latter is a form of fallacy: it doesn't follow from something being natural that it is right. In any case, it is refuted by the existence of various trans-species sexual relations in nature. Arguments around 'human dignity' have similar problems with cultural relativism and often have religious motivations, so are unlikely to convince the non-religious. A stronger and clearer moral argument concerns animal suffering or humans being harmed. Clearly there are moral problems with zoosadistic acts, and even in consensual intercourse there might be problems with the level of informed consent of the animal partner. There are also concerns that certain activities could make the human more likely to engage in violence upon other humans (although cause and effect might be hard to distinguish).

In the case of intercourse with dead cephalopods the strongest argument, the harm argument, breaks down. The cephalopod is already dead and cannot be harmed further (I assume it was not killed specifically for the sex or picture). In addition, cephalopods are very unlikely to have a concern for their posthumous state, so they would not even be harmed if they knew what would happen to their bodies. Squids do not appear to have a higher order desire for privacy or modesty.[2] Diseases are unlikely to spread from invertebrates to humans. The only harm might be the nebulous possibility that the act would have bad psychological effects on the human or on viewers of the picture (for example, by coming to view animals as mere objects), but to my knowledge there is not much evidence for this. It might be grounds for moral concern, but hardly moral condemnation.

Disgust, dignity, and natural order arguments still remain and no doubt drive many to condemn the act, but, as moral reasons go, they appear arbitrary. Where is the distinguishing line between erotic uses of vegetables, sausages, pieces of meat, or squids? I have no doubt some (or perhaps many) conservative people would regard food play as morally problematic for these reasons. But to be consistent they should then argue that erotic uses of (say) cucumbers should be proscribed *as strongly* as squids: trans-kingdom sex is an even greater upset of any natural order (let's ignore the flowers and bees) and would seem to be an even greater challenge to human dignity, and maybe even the dignity of plants![3] If use of a dead animal for sexual gratification is disturbing, what about *parts* of dead animals (meat), cross-species assemblages (sushi), or totally unrecognizable products (sausages)? To a large degree the dignity and natural order arguments seem to be driven by disgust reactions ('that is not supposed to go *there!*') that we have come to recognize as being of little value when judging other sexual practices such as homosexuality.

Disgust is often deeply influenced by framing effects (gelatin becomes unappealing when described as a byproduct of the skin, bones, and connective tissues of animals) and cultural practices (consider your own nation's favourite scare-the-tourists dish). This makes it an unreliable guide for moral truth or edibility: in general it errs on the side of caution. This is effective for avoiding bad food and to keep to local social practices, but it is problematic as a guide for punishing other people in a multicultural world.

If we allow appealing still-life paintings of meat or pictures of people pleasing themselves with sausages, then it seems hard to argue that it is immoral to have pictures of sex with dead cephalopods. We might be concerned about the mental state of people who enjoy them and the welfare of living animals. But we should not allow unreflective disgust to dictate our actions.

## Notes

1. <http://www.theregister.co.uk/2010/05/14/squid_image_charge/>
2. <http://www.practicalethicsnews.com/practicalethics/2010/05/the-privacy-of-the-shrew.html>
3. <http://www.practicalethicsnews.com/practicalethics/2008/04/the-dignity-of.html>

# 52

# NOTHING IS LIKE
# MOTHER'S ICE CREAM

Anders Sandberg

The Icecreamists, an ice cream parlour in Covent Garden, began selling a human milk-based ice cream recently, only to have it confiscated by Westminster Council. The council wanted to check that it was 'fit for human consumption'.[1] New York chef Daniel Angerer was reported serving human cheese[2] (he didn't, but his blog has the recipe[3]). He was advised by the New York Health Department to stop, since they claimed 'cheese made from breast milk is not for public consumption, whether sold or given away'.

What is it exactly that is disturbing about a human milk ice cream or cheese? And are there any good reasons to prevent or impede it from being sold?

## Milk and the harm principle

Westminster Council seemed to invoke the harm principle: it is legitimate to coerce people in order to prevent harm. Breast milk can transmit disease, so it is sensible to check whether the new product is safe. The ice cream makers claim the women their milk comes from have taken the same test used for NHS blood donors and that the milk is pasteurized. If true, the harm principle is not relevant here. Another harm argument would be to claim harm against the donating women. Maybe they get too little compensation? But they were recruited, in the UK case, through the Mumsnet website and voluntarily accepted the price of £15 for 10 ounces.

'It wasn't intrusive at all to donate,' said Victoria Hiley, 35, who responded to the call, 'just a simple blood test. What could be more natural than fresh, free-range mother's milk in an ice cream?'[4]

This doesn't sound like the voice of someone exploited in a serious way.

We would be more concerned if there was a big demand for food milk to compete with the demand from infants; this might threaten the interests of the child. Right now this is not the case. Many lactating mothers complain that their problem is overproduction and they feel guilty about throwing the unneeded milk away. There are many infants in need of milk, of course, but there are no easy ways of redistributing it.

Another objection is that the ice cream would lead to the commodification of motherhood, or of the products of the human body. This concern comes a bit late. There is a thriving market in human hair,[5] not just used for fashion, but also to clean up oil spills and to produce food additives. While sale of human organs is banned in many countries, institutions and companies compensate each other to facilitate transplantations. People donate sperm and blood in exchange for money. Human cheese has been made as an art project. In any case, it is unclear whether there is anything problematic about selling products of the body: we routinely sell our work and mental activity, which are non-material products of our bodies.

## Who has a right to milk?

A different claim is that human milk should always go to humans because they 1) can get the most out of it and 2) it is made for them. But this doesn't seem credible. As already stated, infants cannot consume all the milk (due to overproduction and problems in distributing it to remote but needy infants), so why should others not make use of it?

Were we to accept the argument, however, what implications would it have for our drinking cow's milk? Don't calves have a stronger moral claim to that milk than us? People for the Ethical Treatment of Animals (PETA) actually asked ice cream makers Ben & Jerry in 2008 to make ice cream out of human milk instead of cow's milk,[6] out of concern for animal welfare. In fact, milk willingly given (with full informed consent) might be more ethical than milk forced from cows.

Some might regard eating food made from human products as akin to cannibalism (I do wonder how they view milk-guzzling infants). The moral bad of cannibalism is that it treats others as means rather than ends (especially if they are killed for food) and often contradicts people's posthumous interests. But these are not applicable for this kind of food: nobody is hurt, the donors are not mistreated, and their interests are not harmed.

But we are getting closer to the emotional core of the resistance: disgust.

## The radical indecency of drinking milk

When we think about it, humans drinking cow's milk is actually mildly repulsive. However, it is so useful and has been going on so long, that most of us find it completely natural. We get reminded about the strangeness when we hear about people from other cultures enjoying horse, camel, or moose milk. As J.B.S. Haldane remarked in his classic essay *Daedalus* (1924):

> But if every physical and chemical invention is a blasphemy, every biological invention is a perversion. There is hardly one which, on first being brought to the notice of an observer from any nation which has not previously heard of their existence, would not appear to him as indecent and unnatural.
>
> Consider so simple and time-honored a process as the milking of a cow. The milk which should have been an intimate and almost sacramental bond between mother and child is elicited by the deft fingers of a milk-maid, and drunk, cooked, or even allowed to rot into cheese. We have only to imagine ourselves as drinking any of its other secretions, in order to realise the radical indecency of our relation to the cow.

If we accept trans-species milk drinking as natural, then inter-species milk drinking seems far less problematic. Conversely, if drinking human milk is bad, cow's milk is worse.

We are in the domain of powerful intuitions about what is disgusting, what goes where in the order of things, what substances have some inherent value. Maybe there is a moral assumption in the New York health authorities' claim that human milk is not 'fit for *public* consumption': human milk is something *private*. This would fit with the intuition that it represents a special bond between mother and child, that there is something worrying about selling it and that allowing family members to drink it might be OK while allowing others to do so is not. But this hinges on the assumption that we all agree on what aspects of life should be public or private and that it is a moral matter to agree on where the line should be. While Western culture makes many aspects of life private—such as sex and excretion—the same aspects are not private within other cultures (and the level of privacy has changed over time). In pluralist, democratic societies there will have to be ongoing negotiations about what forms of privacy to enforce or tolerate. There don't seem to be any human universals about what should be in the private or public category; it is hard to believe that something like human milk *must* be private, morally speaking. Of course, public opinion might still be outraged and this might lead to a widely supported ban on human milk food, but we should recognize that this is little more than a choice that can evolve as culture evolves.

This is why appeals to the 'wisdom of repugnance' have such a bad reputation in ethics. If what disgusts us is not a human universal, but highly dependent on culture, then it seems to be problematic as evidence for it being intrinsically harmful or evil. The disgust felt by a racist or homophobe is not good evidence for deciding how to treat others. Human milk food might, by its nature, be close to sensitive areas of our emotions, but there are enough people thinking 'why not?' or even 'beautiful!' about such uses of milk that we should seriously doubt any repugnance-based judgement on the practice.

From a marketing perspective the whole affair has of course been a great success, no matter whether the ice cream goes on sale again. Which raises another question: when is it right to trigger predictable 'yuck!' reactions in order to garner attention?

## Notes

1. <http://www.bbc.co.uk/news/uk-england-london-12615353>
2. <http://nypost.com/2010/03/09/wifes-baby-milk-in-chefs-cheese-recipe/>
3. <http://chefdanielangerer.typepad.com/chef_daniel_angerers_blog/2010/02/mommys-milk.html>
4. <http://www.dailymail.co.uk/news/article-1360225/Shop-sells-breast-milk-ice-cream-London-restaurant-Icecreamists-Baby-Gaga.html>
5. <http://news.bbc.co.uk/1/hi/magazine/8753698.stm>
6. <http://businessethicsblog.com/2008/09/30/human-breast-milk-ice-cream-udderly-ridiculous-right/>

# 53

# RUDENESS AND COLD CALLERS

Hannah Maslen

At 7 pm, as you're eating your dinner, you get a call from an unknown number. You pick it up, half out of curiosity (perhaps your numbers have finally come up on the premium bonds), half out of worry (was a family member likely to have been driving at this time?), but wholly anticipating the interaction that in fact transpires:

'Good evening, I was wondering whether I could talk to [Your Name]?'
'Who's calling?'

Enthusiastically: 'My name's Charlie and I'm calling from Well Known Phone Company Ltd. I wanted to check whether you had thought about updating your tariff? You're due an upgrade.'

You have, in fact, been wondering about updating your tariff, but you're not in the mood to do it now and dinner is getting cold. You think about explaining this to chirpy Charlie, but even an exchange about when you might be free to discuss it feels like an effort.

'We'd be able to save you about...'
'Sorry,' you interject, 'I'm not interested.'
'Understood; if you do ever want to hear about the family-and-friends plan just...'

You hang up, feeling a twinge of guilt and bewildered by how Charlie of Well Known Phone Company Ltd could remain so chirpy in the face of such rejection.

Ordinarily, we tend to think there is a presumption towards being polite to other people. By 'being polite', I mean acting courteously— considering and acknowledging the needs and feelings of others with whom we interact, even when those interactions are very brief and with strangers. If someone follows close behind you through a door, you should pause to keep it open rather than letting it shut in their face. If someone asks you the time, you should at least acknowledge their question. If someone lets you into the traffic, you should indicate your thanks. This presumption towards minimally respectful behaviour arises partly from social convention and partly from our duty to acknowledge that our behaviour can have consequences for others.

Given the presumption towards politeness, how polite must you be to Charlie the salesman? Were you justified in hanging up mid-sentence or was your pang of contrition a sign that you had behaved badly? Or, on a less tolerant day, would you in fact have been justified in expressing anger and contempt towards Charlie?

The presumption of politeness can, of course, be defeated. As a rough sketch: if someone has morally wronged you then you would, depend-ing on the seriousness of the wrong, be justified in displaying a certain level of unfriendliness and criticism towards that person. For example, if someone were to hit you, you would be justified not only in refusing to be civil, but also to blame and remonstrate with that person.

The presumption of politeness can also be defeated if the person with whom you interact has simply been impolite towards you; if they themselves fail to adhere to the particular norms governing minimally respectful behaviour. To offer a very British example, if someone skips a few places in a queue, then the usual etiquette that surrounds waiting alongside other people no longer holds with respect to that person. You would, for example, be justified in not holding open a door for that person.

So, to try to get a handle on how polite you should be to Charlie, we should consider whether Charlie has either done you a moral wrong or failed to be polite himself. Charlie's calling you is unlikely to constitute a moral wrong. In cases of criminal scamming, there is culpable wrong-doing. Charlie, however, does not have such unsavoury intentions—his call is just a bit annoying. The aim of the call might be to persuade you to stay with Well Known Phone Company Ltd, but it would be a stretch to say that, if you agree to update your tariff, you have been exploited. It is also not clear that there is anything particularly destructive of your privacy. You knew that your phone company had your number and you could have simply not answered the call if you feel strongly about only talking to friends and family in the evenings.

But if Charlie has not morally wronged you, has he failed to be polite? Certainly in the demeanour and content of his conversation he has been nothing but civil. Perhaps, then, there is impoliteness displayed by the mere act of calling you. The extent to which this is true will mostly be a matter of etiquette—how socially acceptable it is to call a stranger in the evening—but, when the practice of cold-calling has become so common it seems odd to characterize the simple act of dialling as 'impolite'.

So, if Charlie has not morally wronged you, and if he is adhering to the social norms governing minimally respectful behaviour, should you have seen the conversation with Charlie out? I do not believe so: not because of anything to do with the morality or politeness of the act of calling itself, but instead because of the relation Charlie bears to this act.

In organizational contexts, we can be more or less detached from our roles. In our work, we often do not act as ourselves, pursuing our own goals. Rather, we assume a role or play a part, as defined by the organization. This seems particularly true in the case of call-centre staff. The lines Charlie speaks do not originate from him, but from his role. Focusing on the impersonal nature of the things Charlie says helps us realize that it would be entirely permissible to hang up mid-sentence, with no apology or explanation whatsoever. Despite being polite and energetic, Charlie's requests and responses are not expressive of his own wishes or interests. As a consequence, your refusal to respond politely is entirely permissible. In fact, sincerely apologizing for not wanting to engage in conversation, as if Charlie really wanted to, would be to misconstrue the relation Charlie bears to his role.

However, these same reasons also render it inappropriate to remonstrate with Charlie. Whilst you can hang up, you cannot be outright rude to Charlie, nor take him to task for calling you. Again, to do so would be to attribute his speech to him and erroneously imbue it with sincerity. Charlie, *as Charlie*, is not motivated to have the conversation with you and his words are not really his—they belong to his role. So, whilst it might be *more* permissible to cut off Charlie than it would if he were a person calling of his own volition, it would be *less* permissible to display anger or direct personal insult, given Charlie's lack of sincere self-expression.

As a consequence, there was no need for even a twinge of guilt when you hung up. The implausible chirpiness of Charlie is rendered plausible when we realize that it is not in fact Charlie's chirpiness, but the chirpiness of Well Know Phone Company Ltd, Salesperson #45672.[1]

## Note

1. For further reading, see Dan-Cohen, M. (1991). 'Freedoms of collective speech: a theory of protected communications by organizations, communities, and the state', *California Law Review* 79/5: 1229–67.

# ANIMALS

# 54

# TREATED LIKE ANIMALS

Christine M. Korsgaard

On 5 November 2014, *RT* reported[1] that Filipino workers in Saudi Arabia claimed that they were being 'treated like animals'. On 14 November *The Independent* reported[2] that the members of Pussy Riot complained that while in prison in Russia they were 'treated like animals'. On 17 November the *BBC* reported[3] that Nepalese migrant workers building the infrastructure for the World Cup meeting in Qatar complained of being 'treated like cattle'. On 25 November *The Indian Express* reported[4] that Indian tennis star Sania Merza complained that women in India are 'treated like animals'.

What does it mean to be 'treated like an animal'? The Filipino workers gave as an example that their 'feet were chained'. Members of Pussy Riot complained that in Russian prisons, the wardens 'very casually beat people up. They don't have a sense that they [inmates] are human.' Earlier they claimed that prison administrations 'just treat prisoners as they want with impunity'. By being 'treated like cattle' the Nepalese migrant workers meant 'working up to 12 hours a day, seven days a week, including during Qatar's hot summer months'. On 24 December *Time* reported[5] that the Nepalese migrant workers are dying at the rate of one every two days. Sania Merza said that women in India face discrimination and violence. She also said, 'I hope one day everyone will say that we are equal and women are not treated as objects.'

Merza's last remark raises a question. As these examples suggest, people whose rights are violated; people whose interests are ignored or overridden; people who are abused, harmed, neglected, and unjustly imprisoned, standardly protest that they are being treated 'like animals'. Why do we so often formulate our protest that way, rather than saying, as Merza also said, and as people sometimes do, that we are being treated 'like objects'? After all, it is objects that may, in the words of Pussy Riot, be treated 'just as [we] want with impunity', if indeed anything can. Perhaps it's because people feel that that fails to completely capture the force of their protest. After all, an object cannot suffer from being beaten up or chained or caged, or die from overwork in harsh working conditions. In the relevant sense, you cannot treat an object badly, even if you do treat it 'just as you want with impunity'. But when we treat animals just as we want we can treat them badly. But in that case, the implication of the phrase seems to be that animals are the beings that it is all right to treat badly, and the complainant is insisting that he or she is not one of those.

As Nietzsche pointed out in the *Genealogy of Morals*, we think about moral matters in terms that are borrowed from economics; we say, for instance, that human beings have 'value'. A number of philosophers—Nietzsche himself, Hobbes, and Rousseau, for instance—have tried to trace the idea of human value to economic and social origins, to explain how, psychologically, people came to take the value of their holdings—their land, money, influence, and consequent power—to attach to themselves, to their self-conceptions. Originally, according to these philosophers, to have value was to have high rank, prestige, and privilege. But then the concept took a different turn. For value in the economic sense is relative to supply and demand, and some things—and so, as long as we stay within a conception of value rooted in economics, some people—have more of it than others. Kant argued in the *Groundwork of the Metaphysics of Morals* that moral value isn't like that. Human beings have a value that is not merely relative, a form of 'dignity' which grounds our claims to be treated with respect, but which is not comparative, and which all of us have equally.

But if I'm right about the phrase 'treated like animals', a comparative thought is still at work when we say that. 'You shouldn't treat me that way, for I am not just an animal!' It's as if we were unable to assert our own claims to dignity and respect without invoking a contrast with other creatures who could conceivably be treated with respect, or kindness, or consideration, but, morally speaking—or so we suppose—need not be. It's as if we were unable to affirm our own value without thinking of ourselves as more valuable than someone else. It's as if we thought of our own humanity as the last bastion of rank and privilege.

Is that why we need to deny value to the animals, because that's the only way we can claim it for ourselves? On the contrary: there is no surer sign that a human being understands the nature of his own dignity—his non-comparative value—than the fact that he accords exactly the same value to everyone else. Animals are the sort of thing that can be treated with respect and kindness, and consideration, for some of the same reasons that we are. Of course people shouldn't be treated like animals. But then, neither should animals.

## Notes

1. <http://rt.com/news/saudi-arabia-illegal-migrants-272/>
2. <http://www.independent.co.uk/news/people/pussy-riot-russian-prisoners-are-treated-like-animals-put-in-custody-for-care-9860329.html>
3. <http://www.bbc.com/news/world-middle-east-24980013>
4. <http://blog.practicalethics.ox.ac.uk/2015/01/treated-like-animals-guest-post-by-christine-korsgaard/(http:/indianexpress.com/article/sports/tennis/it-is-difficult-to-be-a-sania-mirza-in-india-says-sania-mirza/>
5. <http://time.com/3646505/world-cup-qatar-nepalese-worker-dying-soccer-football/>

# 55

# WHAT IS A PET WORTH?

Russell Powell

In memory of my pointer mix Casey Jones, my closest friend for more than a decade, and my North Star. The one steady light as I navigated the turbulent seas of degree programs, academic jobs, overseas moves, and intimate relationships. Long May He Run.

Imagine that you leave your sprightly canine companion to the vet for a routine teeth cleaning, only to learn that due to spectacular negligence on the part of the veterinary staff, he was confused for a terminally ill dog and was accidentally 'euthanized'. Imagine another even more horrific scenario, in which a sadistic neighbour steals your feline friend and feeds her to his wood chipper. For the many people who have close relationships with their companion animals, these events would be traumatic and life-altering, evoking a range of moral emotions from profound sadness to uncontainable rage; moral reactions with which many of us could sympathize. It may therefore come as a surprise to some readers to learn that despite the clear moral dimensions of these frightful scenarios, there is little institutional recourse to redress the wrongs that were done.

The reason for this is that in nearly every legal jurisdiction throughout the world, companion animals have the status of ordinary property. And as is the case with all ordinary property, the legal valuation in connection with the loss of a companion animal is indexed to its objective, or market, value. The subjective value of property—i.e. how much one happens to value the item in any given case—is not the relevant legal metric when it comes to determining the appropriate level of compensation for the wrongful loss of property.

As a general principle of tort law, the 'fair market value rule' makes for sensible policy. If my hiking boots are wrongfully damaged, the compensation I receive should be based on what the boots are worth in the marketplace, so that I may replace them and hence be made whole; this valuation should not be affected by the contingent fact that I happen to attach an unusually high value to the boots because, say, they carried me through a spiritual hike in the Himalayas. From a practical legal standpoint, there are simply too many epistemic and procedural difficulties to take subjective, sentimental values into account in making this valuation. Furthermore, allowing recovery for the mawkish value that one happens to attach to one's property, even if this could be reliably determined, may be unfair to the malfeasor who could not have foreseen that such great value would be accorded to the property in question. Therefore both weighty moral and policy-based considerations underpin the fair market value rule.

However, when it comes to the full and fair recovery for the loss of a companion animal, the fair market value rule can lead to unjust legal outcomes. As with other property, the fair market value of a companion animal is determined by how much people are, on average, willing to cough up to purchase a similar animal before they have developed a personal relationship with it. In the case of a mixed breed or older dog or cat, given the superabundance of animals in need of adoption, this sum is close to nil, amounting to no more than, at best, an adoption fee. This means that recovery for wrongful harm to such animals is something in the order of a few hundred dollars. As a result, if one spends thousands of dollars on veterinary bills in an attempt to save the life of a companion animal after it has been wrongfully 'damaged', such expenses are not typically recoverable. This leaves the human caretakers of harmed companion animals effectively without legal recourse and strongly disincentivized to commence an expensive, time-consuming, and emotionally draining lawsuit that can result in only minimal compensation.

While there may be good reason for retaining the common law fair market value rule for ordinary property, this rule is acutely at odds with most people's considered moral intuitions and manifest moral behaviour when it comes to the rightful value of their companion animals. People do not think of their ageing dog as they would an ageing chair—something simply to be replaced when the cost of repair exceeds the sum it would garner in the marketplace. Few veterinary bills would be paid on this rationale. Thinking of our companion animals as simple property is likely to be deeply alienating and morally incomprehensible (and reprehensible) to many people. Surveys show that high proportions of people in developed countries regard their dog and cat companions as members of their family, and this belief is reflected in the significant sums that pet owners spend on the physical and psychological healthcare needs of their pets. Indeed, much of the veterinary industry is premised on the sociological fact that people will spend orders of magnitude more on their pet than their pet is worth under the fair market compensation scheme; yet the vet industry is readily willing to hide beyond the fair market value obstacle to the full and fair recovery for the loss of a companion animal in the case of veterinary negligence or recklessness.

Many people do neglect their pets, of course. But many people also neglect their children, and this fact does not lead us to doubt the value we place on our children when it comes to the civil recovery for the wrongful death or harm to a child. Similarly, the fact that some people continue to treat their dogs or cats as ordinary property with no special moral significance does not undercut the fact that huge numbers of people think and act as if they have strong moral obligations to their companion animals, and think and act as if their companion animals themselves have moral standing. Injuries inflicted on one's companion animal are not regarded solely as personal affronts: 'Hey, you just damaged my minimally valuable property!' is not the reaction we would expect from someone whose beloved dog has been harmed. Rather, such harms evoke sympathies for our animal companion and moral indignation at the wrongdoer that goes well beyond a natural moral aversion to interference with our property rights. The intrinsic (non-instrumental) moral value of sentience is now afforded a central place in European Union principles and is reflected in widespread laws that address animal cruelty and govern the ethics of animal experimentation. Subjectively valuing an inanimate object, such as a pet rock, beyond its market value is rare and could rightfully be considered a sign of moral psychological pathology. In contrast, valuing one's companion dog well beyond its market value is the moral norm in developed societies and, crucially, stems from the *right sorts of moral reasons*—namely, from the fact that we have developed close personal relationships with our pets whom we properly regard as sentient beings, and perhaps even psychological persons, with morally protectable interests. The relationship that many people have with their pets is therefore a deeply moral one. And given the pervasiveness of this psychologically normal and rationally defensible sociocultural pattern, the great value placed on companion animals is eminently foreseeable by malfeasors who negligently, recklessly, or intentionally harm or kill them. It is thus fair to hold such actors accountable for the full damage caused by their wrongful actions.

So what should be done? The legal rules governing civil recovery in the case of harm to companion animals need to be brought in line with contemporary moral thought and behaviour. To this end, some have suggested that courts recognize the legal standing of non-human companion animals, but doing so is highly controversial and may have sweeping legal implications (for, say, the agricultural use of animals) that make judges reluctant to go down this road. Thankfully, there is a less radical way to ensure just compensation and adequate deterrence when it comes to the loss of companion animals. Namely, for common and statutory law to be modified in order to allow for the recovery of emotional distress and/or loss of companionship in connection with the wrongful loss of or injury to a companion animal, just as it currently does for harms to close family members.

Certain non-human companion animals could readily be reclassified as a special class of property without sparking the revolution in animal law that worries jurists. And principles of full and fair recovery in connection with harms to our human families could easily be extended to companion animals in cases where a special family relationship can be amply demonstrated. Indeed, the law has begun to make welcome gestures in this direction.[1] It is high time that the law recognizes the moral value of our closest personal relationships in all their glorious forms, human and otherwise.[2]

## Notes

1. See Sirois, L.M. (2015). 'Recovering for the loss of a beloved pet: rethinking the legal classification of companion animals and the requirements for loss of companionship tort damages', *University of Pennsylvania Law Review* 163: 1199.
2. This piece was inspired by work I did for the Animal Legal Defense Fund with Darren Bernstein, my then fellow Associate of Skadden, Arps, Slate Meagher and Flom, LLP.

# 56

# THE BEST IDEA YOU'VE HEARD ALL YEAR

### Michelle Hutchinson

S cientists from Oxford and Amsterdam have announced the results of an investigation into the environmental impact of growing meat artificially[1] in labs rather than keeping livestock. They found that greenhouse gases would be reduced by up to 96%. Compared to conventional meat, cultured meat would only require 1% of the land and 4% of the water. They estimated that if more resources were put into the research, it would take about five years to produce artificial meat with the consistency of mincemeat, and another five years to produce steaks. Their conclusion is modest: 'We are not saying that we could, or would necessarily want to, replace conventional meat with its cultured counterpart right now.'

But this modesty is misplaced—it should be considered not just desirable, but hugely important to replace conventional with artificial meat.

Think a bit about their amazing feat. We're not just talking about a substitute for meat—a slightly improved kind of Quorn. What they are producing is real meat, with the taste, texture, and nutritional value of meat. And, at a time when climate change is one of the greatest threats we face, they are producing it in a way that radically cuts emissions of harmful gases. Meat production, particularly beef, is one of the major contributors to emissions.[2]

There are other significant benefits of artificial meat. Beef cattle need swathes of land for grazing, leading to deforestation.[3] Lab-grown meat uses just 1% of the land required by animals. Then there's the impact on food prices. Meat is an inefficient source of energy; much more grain is required to feed enough animals to keep people well-fed than would be required if people ate the grain itself. This pushes up the price of grain. Growing meat in a lab reduces the energy used by between 7% and 45%.

Last, but by no means least, is the plight of animals. To push down the price of meat, animals in factory farms are severely mistreated. If we're neither willing to pay enough for meat to allow animals to live adequate lives, nor prepared to become vegetarian, then we ought to take seriously the possibility of replacing factory-farmed animals with meat that can't suffer.

Are there any arguments against producing artificial meat? One is that people might be repulsed by the thought of it. Eating this meat could then be less pleasurable than conventional meat. However, while it is plausible that people would feel an initial sense of revulsion at laboratory meat, the evidence suggests that most of us are adept at ignoring where our food comes from. Almost everyone has a vague idea that the meat they consume involves suffering to animals, but we usually manage not to think about that when we actually sit down for a meal. The chances are that any sense of disgust would quickly abate. In any case, surely the idea that what is on your plate was once alive, deliberately subjected to harm, and then killed, is far less savoury than the idea that it was grown in a laboratory or factory vat?

A second reason for being hesitant about cultured meat is the possibility of its being physically harmful to people. In the past rushing into ingesting new substances back-fired; think of the damage caused by giving Thalidomide to pregnant women. There is strong reason to think that this won't be the case with cultured meat, since what is being produced is not a substitute for meat, but the very substance that we consume all the time. That is not to say that we should not apply rigorous tests to make sure what's being produced is entirely safe.

So the arguments are irresistible. Artificial meat would provide people with the benefits of traditional meat—taste and nutrition—without the attendant suffering to animals. It would make the world a fairer place, since reduced land and water use, as well as reduced emissions, would mean that meat consumption by the rich would no longer cause as much damage to the poor. Ultimately, mitigating climate change and its ensuing problems would benefit everyone.

We should make research into cultured meat a priority.

# Notes

1. <http://www.guardian.co.uk/environment/2011/jun/20/artificial-meat-em issionshttp:/www.ox.ac.uk/media/news_stories/2011/labgrown_meat_would. html>

2. <http://www.lexisnexis.com/uk/nexis/results/docview/docview.do?docLinkInd= true&risb=21_T12247243607&format=GNBFI&sort=BOOLEAN&startDocNo= 1&resultsUrlKey=29_T12247243610&cisb=22_T12247243609&treeMax=true& treeWidth=0&selRCNodeID=5&nodeStateId=411en_GB,1&docsInCategory= 4&csi=158275&docNo=2>

3. <http://www.bbc.co.uk/h2g2/approved_entry/A3556848>

# THE FUTURE AND ITS PEOPLE

# 57

# ENLIGHTENED SURVEILLANCE?

## Stuart Armstrong

We are moving towards a surveillance society. Everywhere. New York City is contemplating using aerial drones for surveillance purposes.[1] North Korea is buying thousands of cameras to spy on its impoverished population.[2] Britain has so many cameras they cease being newsworthy. If increasing surveillance is inexorable—as I think it is—we must ensure that society benefits from this unstoppable trend. We all know the downside of ubiquitous surveillance, but what *good* could come from corporations, governments, and neighbours being able to peer continually into your bedroom (and efficiently process that data)? In the ideal case, how could ubiquitous surveillance work for us?

- **Less crime**. This point is always trotted out by authoritarians, but that doesn't make it any less true. Universal surveillance would dramatically reduce crime and considerably simplify court cases. Instead of interrogating witnesses, simply play the recording. We'll see a reduction in legal hypocrisy (and maybe even in laws). It's hard to ban weed if most people smoke it—and we have the recordings to prove it.
- **Fewer police**. This is the converse advantage. We wouldn't need to maintain a large police force; rational criminals would have to seek honest work and a small rapid reaction force would be enough to deal with the occasional irrational outbreak. Savings in time and money could be made in every aspect of security. If nobody has the privacy to build a bomb, then pat-downs and searches at airports would become redundant.

- **Smaller armies**. As for individuals, so for states. With reliable foreign intelligence, states could reduce their arsenals and their forces—maybe even get rid of nuclear weapons entirely. As long as countries maintained the industrial capacity to re-arm rapidly, if needed, they would be satisfied with a minimal force and a keen eye on their neighbours.
- **Lower risk of private Armageddon**. With total surveillance, there's less chance of a lone individual creating a disaster, through artificial intelligence or *engineered bacteria*.[3]
- **Fewer restrictions on technology**. Many technology restrictions exist to prevent the stupid or dangerous from misbehaving. You can't get hold of semi-dangerous chemicals. There are restrictions on prescribing certain drugs, and so on. These are restrictions all the rest of us have to live with. With total surveillance they would be unnecessary. The dangerous could be stopped individually and the rest of us would be liberated. Similarly, there would be no need for invasive and crippling Digital Rights Management. It would be easy to distinguish those who copied a file merely for private use from those who distributed it publicly.
- **Cut in corruption**. What if we watched the watchers? There would certainly be less corruption and lying among public officials. Attempts by the powerful to shield themselves from surveillance, would quickly become untenable: the holes in the recordings would be blatant, and, in any case, smart algorithms could deduce a lot from the available data.
- **Sousveillance.** We could keep an eye on the politicians and (especially) the corporations whose decisions affect us all, and who often shelter themselves from scrutiny via privacy laws.
- **Epidemiology.** We could track down epidemics as they emerge, quickly establishing the dangerous (or benign) effect of various pollutants. Similarly, we would gain a much better grasp as to which social policies work best and maybe even adjust them in real time.
- **Diluted prejudice.** Often we hate people that we barely know and make unjustified generalizations. In a transparent society, we would be more familiar with members of other groups, and so less likely to feel hostility towards them. And our generalizations would be more accurate.

- **Nicer people!** This is more contentious, but we should consider the possibility that people who know that their words and deeds are recorded, would behave in more pro-social and honest ways. There might be an ever-present risk of enforcing conformity, but the gap between our public and private persona, far from granting us well-needed liberty,[4] may actually condemn our social interactions to hypocrisy and pretence. A high dose of transparency might be just the thing to increase our acceptance of marginal behaviour—we would no longer be able to pretend that it doesn't happen, and would have to embrace and defend it.
- **Romance**. We could pre-screen dubious romantic partners. We currently have a highly unsatisfactory situation. People can, and do, Google their dates, but the information they get is biased and incomplete. Some repeated abusers are not caught, while potential suitors are put off a person who made one embarrassing teenage mistake. More accurate information would allow people both to check for better compatibility and to be more honest about their own desires.
- **No passwords**. This could be the most useful benefit from constant surveillance: no need for passwords or other identifiers. Wherever you go, everything would just know that it's you!

Naturally there are immense dangers as well as benefits to the increase in surveillance, most particularly, concern about creeping totalitarianism. But we'd be lying if we didn't accept that there could be an upside too. And identifying these rewards will at least help us figure out what kind of surveillance society we should be fighting for, if preventing it from emerging is as quixotic as it seems today.[5]

# Notes

1. <http://www.digitaljournal.com/article/341541>
2. <http://www.telegraph.co.uk/news/worldnews/asia/northkorea/9801850/North-Korea-steps-up-surveillance-of-citizens-with-16000-CCTV-cameras.html>
3. <http://en.wikipedia.org/wiki/Synthetic_biology>
4. <http://metapsychology.mentalhelp.net/poc/view_doc.php?type=book&id=2870>

5. For further reading, see: Total surveillance: <https://www.youtube.com/watch?v=zjwzhPkzfpo>; Existential risk: <https://www.youtube.com/watch?v=3jSMeoowGMs>; Making surveillance work: <http://theconversation.com/make-surveillance-work-for-the-people-let-them-spy-back-21634>; Life in the fishbowl: <http://aeon.co/magazine/society/the-strange-benefits-of-a-total-surveillance-state/>

# 58

# WHY IT'S OK TO BLOCK ADS

## James Williams

The practice of 'ad blocking'—the use of specialized software to prevent advertisements from appearing in websites or apps—is under ethical scrutiny.[1]

Arguments against ad blocking tend to focus on the potential economic harms. Because advertising is the dominant online business model, if everyone used ad blockers then wouldn't it all collapse? If you don't see the ads, aren't you getting the services you currently think of as 'free', *actually* for free? Isn't ad blocking, as the industry magazine *AdAge* has called it, 'robbery, plain and simple'?[2]

In response, defenders of ad blocking argue that ads are often annoying and that blocking them is a way to force advertising to improve. Many users object to having data about their browsing and other behaviours tracked by advertising companies. Some also block ads in the hope of speeding up page load times or minimizing data usage.

Remarkably, both sides of this debate simply assume that the large-scale capture and exploitation of human attention is ethical and/or inevitable in the first place. This demonstrates how utterly we have failed to understand the role of attention in the digital age—as well as the implications of spending most of our lives in an environment designed to compete for it.

In the 1970s Herbert Simon pointed out that when information becomes abundant, *attention* becomes the scarce resource. In the digital age, this insight is more relevant than ever.

Think about it: the attention you're deploying in order to read this sentence right now (an attention for which, by the way, I am grateful)— an attention that includes, among other things, the saccades of your eyeballs, the information flows of your executive control function, your daily stockpile of willpower, and the goals you hope reading this will help you achieve—these and other processes you use to navigate your life are literally the object of competition among most of the technologies you use every day. There are literally billions of dollars being spent to figure out how to get you to look at one thing over another; to buy one thing over another; to care about one thing over another. This is the way we are now monetizing the world's information.

The large-scale effort that has emerged to capture and exploit your attention as efficiently as possible is often referred to as the 'attention economy'. In the attention economy, winning means getting people to spend as much time and attention as possible with your product or service. (Although, as it's often said, in the attention economy 'the user is the product'.) Because there's so much competition for people's attention, this inevitably means exploiting the myriad biases that psychologists and behavioural economists have been compiling over the last few decades. In fact, there's a burgeoning industry of authors and consultants helping designers 'hook' users with these methods.

Because we experience the downsides of the attention economy in little drips, we tend to describe them with words of mild bemusement like 'irritating' or 'distracting'. But this is a misreading of their nature. In the short term, distractions can keep us from doing the things we want to do. In the longer term, however, they can accumulate and keep us from living the lives we want to live, or, even worse, undermine our capacities for reflection and self-regulation, making it harder, in the words of Harry Frankfurt, to 'want what we want to want'.[3] Thus there are deep ethical implications lurking here for freedom, well-being, and even the integrity of the self.

Design ethics in the digital age has almost totally focused on how technologies manage our *information*—think privacy, surveillance, censorship, etc. Far less analysis has addressed how our technologies manage our *attention*, and it's long past time to forge new ethical tools for this brave new world.

Think about the websites, apps, or communications platforms you use most. What behavioural metric do you think they're trying to maximize in their design of your attentional environment? What do you think is *actually* on the dashboards in their weekly product design meetings?

Whatever metric you *think* they're nudging you towards, how do you know? Wouldn't you *like* to know? Why *shouldn't* you know? Isn't there an entire realm of transparency and corporate responsibility going undemanded here?

I'll give you a hint, though: it's probably not any of the goals you have for yourself. Your goals are things like 'spend more time with the kids', 'learn to play the zither', 'lose twenty pounds by summer', 'finish my degree'. Your time is scarce and you know it.

Your technologies, on the other hand, are trying to maximize goals like 'time on site', 'number of video views', 'number of page views', and so on. Hence clickbait, hence auto-playing videos, hence avalanches of notifications. Your time is scarce and your technologies know it.

But these design goals are petty and perverse. They don't recognize our humanity because they don't bother to ask about it in the first place. In fact, the design goals often clash with the mission statements of the companies themselves.

Goals of this sort exist largely because they serve the goals of advertising. Most advertising incentivizes design that optimizes for our *attention* rather than our *intentions*. (Where advertising *does* respect and support user intent, it's arguable whether 'advertising' is even the right thing to call it.) Furthermore, because digital interfaces are far more malleable than 'traditional' media ever were, they can be bent more fully to the design logic of advertising.

I often hear people say, 'I use AdBlock, so the ads don't affect me at all.' How head-smackingly wrong they are. (I know, because I used to say this myself.) If you use products and services whose fundamental design logic is rooted in maximizing advertising performance—that is to say, in trying to capture as much of your precious time and attention as possible—then even if you don't see the ads, you still see the ad for the ad (i.e. the product itself). You still get design that uses your psychological biases against you. You still get the flypaper even if you don't get the swatter. A product or service does not magically redesign itself around *your* goals just because you block it from reaching its own.

So if you wanted to cast a vote against the attention economy, how would you do it?

There is no paid version of Facebook. Most websites don't give you the option to pay them directly. Meaningful governmental regulation is unlikely. And the 'attention economy' can't fix itself. Ultimately, the ethical challenge of the attention economy is not one of individual actors, but rather the system as a whole (a perspective Luciano Floridi has termed 'infraethics'[4]).

In reality, ad blockers are one of the few tools that we as users have if we want to push back against the perverse design logic that has cannibalized the soul of the web.

If enough of us used ad blockers, it could help force a systemic shift away from the attention economy altogether, and the ultimate benefit would not just be 'better ads'. It would be better products: better informational environments that are fundamentally designed to be *on our side*, to respect our increasingly scarce attention, and to help us navigate under the stars of our own goals and values. Isn't that what technology is for?

Given all this, the question should not be whether ad blocking is ethical, but whether it is a moral obligation. The burden of proof falls squarely on advertising to justify its intrusions into users' attentional spaces, not on users to justify exercising their freedom of attention.

# Notes

1. See, for example, <http://www.marco.org/2015/08/11/ad-blocking-ethics> and <http://www.bbc.co.uk/news/technology-25219922>
2. <http://adage.com/article/digitalnext/ad-blocking-unnecessary-internet-apoca lypse/300470/>
3. <http://www.jstor.org/stable/2024717>
4. <http://www.ncbi.nlm.nih.gov/pubmed/23197312>

# 59

# WOULD YOU HAND OVER A DECISION TO A MACHINE?

Seán Ó hÉigeartaigh

It's time to take artificial intelligence seriously. Investors are now flocking to AI companies and self-driving cars have gone from sci-fi to near-term development. Commentators have woken up to the prospect that this technology will shortly transform many ways of life.

In January 2015 a conference on the long-term impacts of AI resulted in an open letter, covered in every major newspaper. The letter boldly states: 'we cannot predict what we might achieve when [human] intelligence is magnified by the tools AI may provide, but the eradication of disease and poverty are not unfathomable'.[1] On 28 July 2015, I and others signed the follow-on letter by many of the same AI and robotics researchers calling for a ban on offensive autonomous weapons 'beyond meaningful human control'.[2]

## Making better decisions

Intelligence is a difficult concept to define: in the AI context, the letter relates it to 'the ability to make good decisions, plans, or inferences'. AI systems will not make the remarkable human brain—with its capability for general problem-solving, innovation, and volition—redundant for decades, at a minimum. However, the range of decisions they will make on our behalves will increase, and most decisions—even operational ones—have moral consequences. In many circumstances, AI will make better moral decisions than we do.

Does this sound far-fetched? Consider the 2011 study that showed that Israeli judges on parole hearings are far more lenient after their lunches than before. AI systems won't get tired or hungry.[3] Consider the autonomous battlefield robot, unclouded by fatigue, stress, or fear.

## In the loop

In military ethics, there is extensive debate over the circumstances in which AI systems should operate with a human 'in the loop' and when it should operate entirely autonomously. In many ways, automated systems already have better perception and reflexes than humans, and are slowed down by human input. The human added value comes from our judgement and decision-making, but these are not infallible.

As Georgetown Law Professor (and former Pentagon official) Rosa Brooks provocatively put it, the US's record on kill decisions in combat scenarios is 'horrible'. The real question is whether it's ethical to stop machines from making decisions 'when they're going to do it better than we will.'[4]

Human judgement added to the loop may prove to be an impairment rather than a safeguard.

## Trusting the machine

In given, limited situations (for example, a medical treatment decision, a decision on how to allocate a project's budget most efficiently, or a decision on whether an incoming target constitutes an enemy combatant) it's likely that we will soon have AI able to weigh up the facts, and make a decision as good or better than a human's 99.99% of the time. Machine decisions will be unclouded by bias and based on vastly more information.

Some people are instinctively nervous about subcontracting moral decisions to machines. But we already find it natural to trust other humans to make moral decisions on our behalf. We don't have the time, opportunity, or skillset to make sound, morally informed decisions about everything that we affect. We allow lawmakers, judges, and juries to design and apply the moral codes by which our society operates. We elect politicians who decide how much of our taxes should go on support for the poor, healthcare, and renewable-energy subsidies. In our everyday lives, we allow friends and colleagues to guide us or act for us in myriad ways.

So why not trust the machine? There are actually several good reasons to be wary.

True, human decision-making is riddled with biases and inconsistencies, but our inconsistencies are relatively predictable. We know how to account for them. And there are limits to how nonsensical an intelligent, balanced person's 'wrong' decision will be, due to the vague, currently uncomputable concept we call 'common sense'.

This is not necessarily the case with AI. When AI is 'wrong', it can be spectacularly wrong, with more unpredictable outcomes. Simple algorithms should be extremely predictable, but can make bizarre decisions in 'unusual' circumstances. A trivial example: in 2011, two very basic pricing algorithms—one programmed to sell a book a shade cheaper than its nearest competitor, the other to sell a book at a considerably higher price than its competitors—kept automatically pushing each other's prices up, to the point where a textbook was being sold on amazon for $23 million.[5] Less trivially, unusual circumstances (concerns over European debt crisis leading to unusual algorithmic stock sales), and a cascade of unexpected interactions between high-frequency trading algorithms played a key role in wiping a trillion dollars off the US stock market during the 2010 Flash Crash.[6]

As the decision-making processes become more complicated and the sets of actions that result from them less intuitive, it becomes ever harder even for technically skilled people to tell at a glance if the reasoning behind the decisions is sound, provided the results turn out well the vast majority of the time. The upshot is that we simply have to 'trust' the methods more and more. It also becomes harder to figure out how, why, and in what circumstances the machine will go wrong, and what the magnitude of the failure will be.

## Machines we understand and that understand us

This calls for urgent research. One challenge is technical: we design the things, although to foresee every circumstance in which the AI might make decisions, and what might possibly go wrong, is hugely difficult. But there is scope for thinking carefully about safeguards and ways to limit the extent of failure. And research is being proposed for ways to make the internal processes of techniques like neural networks[7] more easily interrogated by human users.

The second challenge is the human side. For all but the most technically proficient user, these systems are 'black boxes'—we can see the inputs and outputs, but without a clear sense of the internal workings. Therefore, we need to understand the limitations of these black boxes clearly. And we need to make sure we have the skills to make decisions effectively when the AI systems encounter a scenario they can't cope with, even if we rarely have cause to intervene. The aviation industry calls a version of this challenge 'the autopilot problem', where over-reliance on the autopilot can result in human pilots lacking the understanding needed to respond correctly to flight problems (as, for example, in 2009 when, after the autopilot disconnected, human pilot error resulted in Flight 447 crashing with the loss of all on board).[8]

The third intersects philosophy and computing: as we progress towards more powerful, more general AI, with the eventual goal of 'strong' AI—artificial intelligence functionally equivalent to a human's (or greater) across all intellectual domains that we care about—it will be essential to find ways to imbue AI systems with motivations that encompass the shared values of humans comprehensively and reliably. In other words, we want to design machines that may become smarter than us as they sidestep the many limitations of biology, but will still act in our best interests. This is easier said than done though, as human values are incredibly complex, often inconsistent, and by no means universal. While Asimov's laws of robotics appeal, their drawbacks are obvious after a little thought.[9] Designing such a powerful technology safely and beneficially for humanity may be the greatest challenge of all.[10]

# Notes

1. The AI open letter is available at: <http://futureoflife.org/misc/open_letter>
2. The autonomous weapons open letter is available at: <http://futureoflife.org/AI/open_letter_autonomous_weapons>
3. Danziger, S., Levav, J., and Avnaim-Pesso, L. (2011). 'Extraneous factors in judicial decisions', *Proceedings of the National Academy of Sciences* 108/17: 6889–92. <http://www.pnas.org/content/108/17/6889.full>

4. Transcript of *Looking Forward: US National Security Beyond the Wars*. (12 June 2013). Centre for a New American Security. <http://www.cnas.org/files/multimedia/documents/Transcript-%20Bugs%20Bytes%20&%20Bots_1.pdf>

5. <http://www.digitaltrends.com/computing/why-did-amazon-charge-23698655-93-for-a-textbook/>

6. See Bostrom, N. (2014). *Superintelligence: Paths, Strategies, Dangers* (Oxford: Oxford University Press), p. 16–17.

7. Neural networks are a very powerful set of techniques that are responsible for many of the recent advances in machine learning. However, due to their design (consisting with many layers of interconnecting nodes, with up to billions of weighted parameters), it can be difficult for even their programmers to figure out exactly how their results are being generated. See: <http://www.nature.com/nature/journal/v521/n7553/pdf/nature14539.pdf>

8. <http://www.bloomberg.com/news/articles/2011-05-26/air-france-crash-pits-pilot-brains-against-computers-taking-over-cockpits> <https://en.wikipedia.org/wiki/Air_France_Flight_447>

9. 'Rule 1: A robot must not harm a human, or through inaction, allow a human to come to harm.' But what constitutes harm? Should a robot prevent a human from eating an unhealthy hamburger? And should a robot prevent a human from eating an expensive meal, when that money saved could save another human life elsewhere in the world?

10. For further reading, see Singer, P. W. (2009). *Wired for War: The Robotics Revolution and Conflict in the 21st Century* (London: Penguin).

# 60

# SHOULD WE BE ERASING MEMORIES?

S. Matthew Liao, Anders Sandberg,
and Julian Savulescu

There is a haunting turn of phrase that comes up again and again in the testimony of those who have suffered or witnessed terrible crimes:

> I wish I could forget.

One child, whose rapist was sentenced to 15–18 years in Florida in 2014, told the court:

> I wish I could forget and have a new brain, so I don't remember.[1]

Another woman who survived a violent sexual assault said:

> Days after, my scars were healing on the outside, but the memories hurt just as bad because no matter what I tried, I couldn't get them out of my mind...I will always have a constant reminder for the rest of my life of the one night I wish I could forget.[2]

Likewise, the terrible burden of memory weighs heavily on returning soldiers, many of whom suffer flashbacks to those memories as a symptom of Post Traumatic Stress Disorder (PTSD):

> Much of it was very frightening...Some of which I wish I could forget and I cannot.[3]

For many, these memories will be a lifelong sentence. One 94-year-old veteran of the D-Day invasion said:

It's still in my memory. Sometimes I wish I could forget but I can't.[4]

Increasingly, scientists are uncovering new ways of manipulating memories. For instance, one research team found that raising the enzyme levels of PKMzeta—a molecule thought to be needed for strengthening the connections between brain cells—enhanced a rodent's ability to remember, while blocking the enzyme resulted in the erasure of a particular memory.[5] Another research team found that when the drug Latrunculin A was injected into a rodent's amygdala—the brain region responsible for emotions—certain memories can be selectively erased while other memories are left intact.[6] Using optogenetics—a technique that uses light to manipulate and study nerve cells that have been sensitized to light—a third research team found that unpleasant memories in rodents can be neutralized and/or even re-associated with more positive emotions.[7]

Such research raises hope for treating conditions such as PTSD, in which painful memories become intrusive and damage an individual's ability to live an ordinary life. While we are still some distance away from being able to achieve this, it's possible that within the next decade we will be able to control the erasing of memory.

Forgetting is, of course, an ordinary and important part of life. Forgetting painful events is important to our psychic happiness. Indeed, even self-deception may be important for maintaining psychological stability. Just imagine if we really saw ourselves as others saw us! Still, using memory-modifying technologies (MMTs) to reduce the negative effects of trauma raises a variety of normative issues.[8]

It is unlikely that anybody could successfully erase the knowledge of an important personal tragedy, since evidence that it happened will usually be distributed among family, friends, and society at large. But there are falsehoods we could end up believing as well as forms of self-deception. This might have damaging consequences. A soldier who forgot what he did during a war (or even that he participated in the war) would get a nasty shock if presented with evidence of his past, especially if it conflicted with the identity he had created for himself. The soldier might also hold erroneous beliefs about his courage or cruelty, traits that might be relevant in a crisis situation.

It is, however, worth recognizing that our identities are amazingly fluid and inconsistent even today. Psychological studies have shown that a surprising number of our own memories—even about key autobiographical facts—are actually incorrect in some details or outright false. If we think truthfulness of memories is very important, we should already be concerned. Perhaps the open use of MMTs will have the beneficial effect of making people more sceptical about the veracity of their memories. Moreover, if facing up to reality is important, then perhaps we should intervene to prevent natural memory erasure, to improve memory in those who forget too easily. Unless we all have exactly the right amount and accuracy of recall—highly unlikely—the issue of memory modification will have to be addressed.

Another normative issue concerns appropriate moral reactions: there may be more and less appropriate ways of responding to significant events. Suppose that you are hit by a drunk driver and given a treatment at the hospital to soften the emotional memory. Later you re-encounter the driver. Looking back at the event you feel that it was a bad event, but you don't feel the anguish that you would have otherwise felt. When the driver asks for forgiveness, there is a risk that you would forgive him too easily. Forgiveness is an important moral act that requires us to overcome our indignation or resentment for the sake of our moral values or personal commitments. A failure to feel such emotions may preclude genuine forgiveness.

Being able to modify our memories may affect our moral and legal obligations. In particular, memories may serve as evidence, not only for oneself, but for others. For example, Neil Armstrong's memory of landing on the moon, a Holocaust victim's memory, or a statesman's memory of what he did in office, may not just be evidence for them, but also for the rest of the world. Some of these memories might be so important to others that there is a duty to remember them, a duty that could not be met if they were altered by MMTs.

For most of us, the point of using memory modification will be to enhance our personal well-being. People should enjoy liberty to use these kinds of technologies unless they harm other people. The real problems regarding MMTs might be the risk of subtle self-harm. In particular, the inappropriate use of MMTs can deny access to important truths, reduce our self-knowledge, and prevent us from satisfying our obligations to ourselves and to others. But MMTs could also be used to enrich our lives by reducing unnecessary pain or enhancing the memories that truly make us unique individuals. Correct application of MMTs requires understanding the role of memories in a person. It also requires that we understand what a good life for a human being is, and the role of memory in that life.

# Notes

1. <http://www.gazettenet.com/home/11398328-95/richard-meyer-of-cummington-sentenced-to-15-18-years-in-state-prison-for-sexually-assaulting>
2. <http://nypost.com/2015/06/18/rape-victim-details-chilling-ordeal-at-attackers-sentencing/>
3. <http://www.wiscnews.com/news/local/article_b7b3c324-c7ec-11e2-9e1e-0014bcf887a.html>
4. <http://www.knoxnews.com/news/state/pair-of-greene-countians-among-dwindling-number-of-d-day-veterans>
5. <http://www.livescience.com/13063-molecule-memory-enhance-erase-110203.html>
6. <http://www.scientificamerican.com/article/memories-of-meth-can-be-deleted>
7. <http://www.nature.com/nature/journal/v513/n7518/full/nature13725.html>
8. <http://link.springer.com/article/10.1007%2Fs12152-008-9009-5?LI=true>

# 61

# ADDING HAPPY PEOPLE

Theron Pummer

Almost every week there's a headline about our planet's population explosion. For instance Indian officials confirmed recently[1] that India is projected to overtake China in just over a decade to become the most populous country on Earth. Many are worried that the planet is becoming increasingly overpopulated. Whether it is overpopulated, underpopulated, or appropriately populated is a challenging ethical question.

Let's suppose a 'happy life' is one that would be on balance well worth living from the point of view of the person living it. Is it *good* to add people with happy lives to the world? This question divides into two more specific ones. First, is it good to add happy people, in virtue of the good effects of doing so for us already existing people? Second, is it good to add happy people, independently of any effects on the already existing? The latter question is by far the more intriguing.

The Canadian philosopher Jan Narveson famously answered this question in the negative, saying: 'We are in favour of *making people happy*, but neutral about *making happy people*.'[2] Whether this stance is correct has a wide range of practical implications for procreation, resource conservation, climate change, and existential risks (such as the danger of a large asteroid colliding with the planet). Some of the implications are profound: since there are *very* many happy future people who could exist, if morality were in favour of making happy people we'd have an overwhelmingly strong reason to pursue the colonization of other planets by our descendants; we'd have very little, if any, reason to do this if Narveson were right.

But I think Narveson is wrong. In addition to being about making people happy, morality *is* about making happy people. By adding happy people we *in one way* make the world a better place and we have significant reason to do so. This significant reason would entail that we *should* add happy people, if there were absolutely no downside to doing so. Of course, it may be that adding many happy people to the current population of Earth would have serious environmental and social downsides, and be a bad thing *all things considered*.

Instead, suppose I could push a button that would create billions of happy people living on several large and lush Eden-like planets. These people would in turn produce further generations of happy people, who would do likewise, and so on for the foreseeable future. Pushing the button would cost me nothing and do no harm or wrong. Would it be wrong of me *not* to push the button, in this case? Yes, I believe it would.

There are several arguments that philosophers have offered in favour of adding happy people. I'll sketch just two.

The most fascinating argument is based on a kind of scepticism about the moral significance of the boundaries between persons, according to which persons are, at most, mere containers of what really matters: *happiness*. On this view, it doesn't matter in and of itself where a fixed amount of happiness is placed. Whether we put it in this or that container, or build a new container to put it in, is in itself irrelevant. Thus, on this view, making people happy and making happy people are equally morally important, other things being equal.

There are different routes to such scepticism about the moral significance of the boundaries between persons. One is purely metaphysical: there simply *are* no separate persons; there are only sets of experiences. There's a set of experiences here where this chapter is being written, and another set over there, and there, where it's being read. But there are no entities above and beyond these experiences, who *have* them. This sort of view is advocated by Buddhists as well as the eighteenth-century Scottish philosopher, David Hume. Another route is only 'metaphysically inspired', and is consistent with the belief that there really are separate persons. The idea here is that when we study certain challenging cases within the literature on the metaphysics of persons and personal identity,[3] it appears very difficult to maintain the moral significance of these notions, either in general or within particular parts of morality. One such case is that of personal *fission*: it is stipulated that a person would survive if she lost either of her cerebral hemispheres, but what in fact happens is her two hemispheres come apart and each is successfully transplanted into its own 'fresh' body. A powerful argument has been made that this reveals that identity is not what really matters—the two resulting persons are clearly not identical with each other and it seems arbitrary to claim that one of them is identical to the original person.[4]

But the most fascinating sort of argument in favour of adding happy people isn't, in my estimation, the most compelling one. Suppose we grant that it matters whether some amount of happiness is located in the life of an already existing person rather than that of a merely possible person. Still, a simple and plausible thought is that adding happiness is good to some extent, wherever it's placed. It seems even harder to resist when viewed in light of the analogous thought about suffering: that adding suffering is bad to some extent, wherever it's placed. Surely it would be bad to bring into the world a life of relentless and insufferable pain. Several philosophers have attempted to defend the following asymmetry: while it's bad to add suffering by adding miserable people, it's *not* good to add happiness by adding happy people. In my view, none of these attempts succeeds.[5]

Largely because I think the asymmetry can't be defended adequately, I also think the world would, in one way, be made better by the addition of happy people to it. I believe we have reason to colonize a variety of planets throughout the galaxy, bringing about trillions of happy lives. Indeed, I believe we have *a lot* of reason to pursue this; about as much reason as we'd have to prevent trillions of miserable lives from coming into existence.

# Notes

1. <http://articles.economictimes.indiatimes.com/2015-05-05/news/61833343_1_population-growth-decadal-growth-rate-family-planning>
2. *The Monist* (1973). 'Moral problems of population' 57/1: 62–86; quote on p. 80.
3. Noonan, H. (2003). *Personal Identity*, second edition (London: Routledge).
4. Derek Parfit is among the first to explore the metaphysically inspired route, using cases like this one. See Part Three of (1984). *Reasons and Persons* (Oxford: Oxford University Press). A natural response is that fission cases reveal psychological or physical continuity to be what matters (rather than identity). Jacob Ross impressively challenges this move in his (2014). 'Divided we fall:

fission and the failure of self-interest', *Philosophical Perspectives* 28/1: 222–62. For a puzzle about fission and desert, see my (2014). 'Does division multiply desert?' *Philosophical Review* 123/1: 43–77.

5. For example, Roberts, Melinda (December 2011). 'The asymmetry: a solution', *Theoria* 77/4: 333–67.

# 62

# THE PREGNANT MAN AND OTHER CONCEPTUAL SURPRISES

Guy Kahane

We should all know what it means to be a parent, a father, or a mother. Those who aren't themselves parents all have, or have had, parents. In fact, calling out to your mother or father may have been your first word. And what could be simpler than something that can be grasped by a baby?

When we are told that a person is some child's mother or father, we usually assume that this is the person that conceived the child and is now raising it; if this is a woman, we also assume that she gave birth to the child. But we learn early on that this needn't be the case: there are, after all, stepparents and foster parents and adoptive parents (as well as cuckolded ones...). A child's biological parents needn't be the ones who raise it, and vice versa. There is a temptation to ask, in such cases, whether someone is the 'real' father or mother, but this isn't a useful question. To conceive and give birth to a child, and to raise and be responsible for it, are two different things. Our ordinary concept of a parent just assumes they go together. And they normally do, but they don't have to.

Once we draw the distinction between biological parenthood and the role of raising a child, new possibilities become visible and we can ask questions we couldn't have asked otherwise. For example, why is it that most of us want to be the biological parents of the children we raise, when there are already so many children out there that we could raise instead? Or, with Plato and some Israeli Kibbutzes, do children really need to be raised by parents of any kind?

That the biological parents of a child don't also need to be those who raise it is, of course, nothing new. But recent advances in medicine and technology are forcing us to rethink what we mean by 'biological parent', since it turns out that this concept also refers to a bunch of different things; things that until now have always gone together, but no longer need to. Some of this is already familiar: the mother who conceived a child, for example, needn't also be the one carrying it to term, and the sperm that conceives a child may come from an anonymous donor. But some newer variations on biological parenthood still have the power to surprise and even to shock.

In one recent court case in Israel, a lesbian couple, one member of which donated an egg for insemination while the other carried the child to term, petitioned the Tel Aviv Family Court to receive joint recognition as the child's biological parents. The women were married in a Jewish Conservative ceremony and had undergone the joint parenting process with the Health Ministry's approval. But the Interior Ministry refused to register them both as the child's biological parents. In their petition, the couple claimed that the biological and legal right to parenthood is a fundamental human right, and that it is in the child's best interest to be legally recognized as the biological son of both his birth mother and her partner. However, Israel's Attorney General strongly objected to the whole notion of 'joint biological parenthood', denying that there could be more than one biological mother. He recommended that only the birth mother be recognized as the child's parent, and that the egg donor settle for formal adoption.

This is confused. In the old sense of the word, neither of the two women is the biological mother. In such cases it is pointless to ask who is the 'real' biological mother. But we can easily change this concept so that both women would count as biological mothers. And why shouldn't we?

A similar issue is raised by a controversial new procedure known as mitochondrial donation. This is a variation on in-vitro fertilization (IVF) in which, in order to prevent inherited mitochondrial diseases, the mitochondrial DNA of the created embryo comes from a third party. There is a straightforward sense that the resulting child has three biological parents: one father and two mothers (although since little of the genetic make-up of the child comes from the 'mitochondrial mother', her contribution is, in this sense, less important).

Finally, there is the tabloid favourite, Thomas Beatie, the world's first pregnant man,[1] who turned out to be a woman who identifies as male and has had a sex change operation (in fact, the operation only involved the removal of breast glands to flatten his chest). Thomas Beatie's wife, Nancy, apparently inseminated him using sperm from an anonymous donor, after first being refused medical assistance by eight different doctors. In an interview Beatie said, 'It's not a male or female desire to have a child.' 'It's a human desire. I have a very stable male identity.' And Mrs Beatie explained that, 'He's going to be the father and I'm going to be the mother.'

Wittgenstein long ago argued that many of our concepts presuppose certain contingent background conditions. There aren't many concepts more central to our form of life than the concepts of father and mother. And in their everyday use these concepts really do presuppose so much: mundane facts about reproduction and gender and child development and human attachment. But these assumptions can no longer simply be taken for granted. When Thomas Beatie bears a child, will he be the father or the mother? Could a child have two biological mothers? Does this even matter?

It is useful here to distinguish between two kinds of concepts. On the one hand, there are what philosophers call 'thin' concepts: concepts like well-being, rights, duty, or dignity. These concepts are highly abstract and general, and don't assume any very elaborate background context of empirical facts and social practices. By contrast, the concepts of father and mother are much 'thicker' concepts: concepts that in their ordinary use presuppose a great deal of empirical background and also have a very rich evaluative dimension. These concepts are associated with more than bare labels or roles; they are also the focus of a range of distinctive emotions, patterns of behaviour, and practices.[2]

There is a perfectly good sense in which 'thin' concepts have an ethical priority. If there are rights, then any plausible ethical theory would need to put rights at its centre. Thicker concepts like mother or father are not fundamental in *that* way. Not all conceivable societies need them. It's not that difficult to conceive of a society in which there are no parents, and it is not even hard to come up with a science fiction scenario in which people come into existence without having biological parents of any kind. Because thin ethical concepts are more basic in this way, we can use them to assess the kind of possibilities that our thicker concepts foreclose, or at least conceal. What does it matter, we think, whether Thomas Beatie is a father or mother, biological or adoptive, so long as the child will be healthy and happy. And so long as no one is harmed, people should have a right to shape their life in whatever way they see fit. If we need to revise our old concepts, or even drop them and come up with new ones, who cares?

Of course it is not so easy to say how the long-term life of Beatie's future child will be affected by the distinctive circumstances of its family—the Beaties are engaging in what J. S. Mill called 'experiments in living'.[3] But there is no special reason to think that this 'experiment' will not go well. Still, as we see more such 'experiments' (some will go better than others), the empirical background that has so far sustained practices like that of parenthood will no longer be obvious, putting pressure on some central concepts. Nothing prevents us from revising and updating our concepts. We can start to think of parenthood as a legal matter, as a cluster of duties and rights, determined by, say, considerations about the interests of existing and future people (there is already a move in this direction).

The problem is that as we move from 'thick' to 'thin', we lose some of the richness that is needed to sustain a meaningful life. And this can lead to tension. Think of the controversy about gay marriage. Many gay couples do not want just the legal status of a civil union. They want the full 'thick' thing, with all of its associations and resonance and history. The Beaties and the Israeli lesbian couple do not just want to be legal parents—they want to be father and mother (or mother and mother). Barack Obama, who barely knew his biological father, has written a book called *Dreams from My Father*. Nobody would write a book called *Dreams from My Legal Guardian*.

So we have, on the one hand, a move towards legalized, thin conceptions of relations between humans, and, on the other, still powerful desires and needs expressed in terms of the older, thicker notions. The two can co-exist, at least for a while. But ultimately, they may not be compatible.

Biology excludes certain possibilities and many of our core concepts grow to reflect that. The way things have always been seems like the way they must be. But then technology intervenes, and we discover that we need to change the way we think and talk to accommodate new options: things that we unthinkingly assumed to always go together can come apart, and can be mixed and matched in surprising ways. And this means we now have more options to choose from and therefore greater freedom. It also means that instead of blindly accepting the way things happen to be, we can identify ways in which the natural order, and the concepts that reflect it, may block certain paths to human flourishing, or reinforce various forms of injustice. That is to say, things would be getting better; better in the 'thin' sense. But at the same time, something is still lost: a 'thicker' way of living and thinking that may be contingent and optional and highly nebulous, but which also helps give content and meaning to our lives. Progressives often see things as getting better and better. Conservatives complain that things keep getting worse. There is a sense in which both are right.

# Notes

1. <http://news.bbc.co.uk/1/hi/world/americas/7330196.stm>
2. The distinction between 'thin' and 'thick' comes from the work of the anthropologist Cleeford Geertz, and I use these terms more or less in Geertz's sense. Within moral philosophy, these terms are usually understood in a slightly narrower sense. See Bernard Williams's classic book (2006). *Ethics and the Limits of Philosophy* (London: Routledge).
3. <http://www.utilitarianism.com/ol/three.html>

# NOTES ON CONTRIBUTORS

**Stuart Armstrong's** research at the Future of Humanity Institute centres on existential risks, the risks and possibilities of artificial intelligence, the long-term potential for intelligent life, and anthropic (self-locating) probability.

**Allen Buchanan** is Professor at Duke University and King's College London Law School.

**Steve Clarke** is Associate Professor at the Centre for Applied Philosophy and Public Ethics, Charles Sturt University, in Australia, and Senior Research Associate of the Oxford Uehiro Centre for Practical Ethics. He is the author of *The Justification of Religious Violence* (Wiley-Blackwell, 2014) and co-editor of *The Ethics of Human Enhancement: Understanding the Debate* (Oxford University Press, 2016).

**Tony Coady** is an Australian philosopher, well known for his writings on epistemology and on issues concerning political morality. He is Emeritus Professor of Philosophy at the University of Melbourne. His publications include *Testimony: A Philosophical Study* (Oxford University Press, 1992), *Morality and Political Violence* (Cambridge University Press, 2008), and *Messy Morality: The Challenge of Politics* (Oxford University Press, 2008).

**Lachlan de Crespigny** is a retired obstetrician and gynaecologist based in Australia. He has a special interest in ethics.

**Roger Crisp** is Uehiro Fellow and Tutor in Philosophy at St Anne's College, Oxford, and Professor of Moral Philosophy at the University of Oxford. He is author of *Mill on Utilitarianism, Reasons and the Good* and *The Cosmos of Duty: Henry Sidgwick's Methods of Ethics,* and has translated Aristotle's *Nicomachean Ethics* (Cambridge University Press).

**Katrien Devolder** is Marie Curie Senior Research Fellow in the Oxford Uehiro Centre for Practical Ethics and at Wolfson College, Oxford. She trained in philosophy at Ghent University and the Université libre de Bruxelles. She has published books on cloning (Leuven University Press, 2001) and embryonic stem-cell research (Oxford University Press, 2015), and is currently working chiefly on the ethics of medical complicity in torture, unethical research, and objectionable social norms.

**Tom Douglas** trained in clinical medicine at the University of Otago, New Zealand, before coming to Oxford as a Rhodes Scholar in 2003. He is now

Senior Research Fellow in the Oxford Uehiro Centre for Practical Ethics and Golding Fellow at Brasenose College. His work focuses mainly on the ethics of using medical technologies for non-medical purposes, such as cognitive enhancement, criminal rehabilitation, and moral improvement.

**Brian D. Earp** is Research Associate at the Oxford Uehiro Centre for Practical Ethics. He holds degrees from Yale, Oxford, and Cambridge universities with training in cognitive science, psychology, philosophy, and ethics. He is also a contributing writer for the *Atlantic* magazine as well as a multiple award-winning professional actor and singer.

**David Edmonds** is a BBC journalist and author of many philosophy books, including (with J. Eidinow) *Wittgenstein's Poker* and, most recently, *Would You Kill the Fat Man?* (Princeton University Press). With Nigel Warburton he co-runs *Philosophy Bites* (http://www.philosophybites.com) which has had 29 million downloads.

**Kyle T. Edwards** received her doctorate from Oxford where she was jointly at the Ethox Centre and the Uehiro Centre for Practical Ethics. Her dissertation examined the role of bioethics in UK regulation of emerging biotechnologies in the areas of assisted reproduction, genetics, and drugs and devices. She is now at Yale Law School.

**Jim A.C. Everett** is a PhD student in the Department of Experimental Psychology at Oxford, and Research Associate in the Department of Philosophy.

**Cécile Fabre** is Senior Research Fellow at All Souls College, Oxford. She has written extensively on social justice, democracy, and, more recently, war ethics. Her books include *Government and the Decent Life*, *Whose Body is it Anyway?*, and *Cosmopolitan War* (Oxford University Press). Her latest book is *Cosmopolitan Peace* (Oxford University Press, 2016).

**Charles Foster** is Fellow of Green Templeton College, Oxford, Senior Research Associate at the Oxford Uehiro Centre for Practical Ethics, Research Associate at the Ethox and Helex centres, and a member of the University of Oxford Faculty of Law. Recent books include *Altruism and Welfare in the Law* (Springer, 2015), *Human Dignity in Bioethics and Law* (Hart Publishing, 2011), *The Laws and Ethics of Dementia* (Hart Publishing, 2014), *Medical Law: A Very Short Introduction* (Oxford University Press, 2013), and *Choosing Life, Choosing Death* (Hart Publishing, 2009). He is currently working on books about depression and about the use of intuitions in ethical reasoning.

**Lynn Gillam** is an academic director and clinical ethicist at the Children's Bioethics Centre at the Royal Children's Hospital, and Professor in Health Ethics at the School of Population and Global Health at the University of Melbourne.

**Hilary Greaves** is Associate Professor of Philosophy at the University of Oxford. Her research spans many areas of ethical theory, especially utilitarian and consequentialist theory, and issues lying at the interface of ethics and economics.

**Chris Gyngell** is Marie Skłodowska-Curie Fellow with the Uehiro Centre for Practical Ethics. His research interests lie primarily in bioethics, moral theory, and the philosophy of health and disease.

**Anders Herlitz** is COFAS Marie Curie Post-doctoral Research Fellow at the Department of Philosophy, Rutgers University, and a researcher at the Department of Philosophy, Linguistics and Theory of Science, University of Gothenburg.

**Kei Hiruta** is Research Fellow in the Faculty of Philosophy, University of Oxford, and Junior Research Fellow at Wolfson College, Oxford. His research lies at the intersection of political philosophy and intellectual history, with particular interest in the idea of freedom and its history.

**Michelle Hutchinson** completed her PhD in Applied Ethics at Oxford University. Her work focuses on how we should prioritize within global health. She runs Giving What We Can, an international non-profit that moves money to the most effective charities tackling extreme poverty.

**Guy Kahane** is Deputy Director of the Uehiro Centre for Practical Ethics, Oxford, and Associate Professor in the Faculty of Philosophy at Oxford University. Kahane is also Fellow and Tutor in Philosophy at Pembroke College, Oxford, and Associate Editor of the *Journal of Practical Ethics*.

**Andreas Kappes** has a PhD in social psychology and was Post-doctoral Fellow at New York University and University College before going to Oxford to work at the Department of Experimental Psychology and the Uehiro Centre for Practical Ethics. Using psychological and neuroscientific methods, he studies decision-making and learning with an emphasis on the social and moral domain.

**Christine M. Korsgaard** is Arthur Kingsley Porter Professor of Philosophy at Harvard University, and author of *Creating the Kingdom of Ends* (Cambridge University Press, 1996), *The Sources of Normativity* (Cambridge University Press, 1996), *The Constitution of Agency* (Oxford University Press, 2008), and *Self Constitution: Agency, Identity, and Integrity* (Oxford University Press, 2009).

**Seth Lazar** is Senior Research Fellow at the School of Philosophy, Australian National University, and author of *Sparing Civilians* (Oxford University Press, 2015).

**Neil Levy** is Deputy Director (Research) of the Oxford Centre for Neuroethics, and a professor of philosophy at Macquarie University, Sydney. His books include *Neuroethics* (Cambridge University Press, 2007), *Hard Luck* (Oxford University Press, 2011), and *Consciousness and Moral Responsibility* (Oxford University Press, 2014).

**S. Matthew Liao** is Director and Associate Professor in the Center for Bioethics, and Affiliated Professor in the Department of Philosophy at New York University. He is the author of over 40 articles and the monograph *The Right to Be Loved* (Oxford University Press, 2015), and editor of *Moral Brains: The Neuroscience of Morality* (Oxford University Press, 2014), *Philosophical Foundations of Human Rights* (Oxford University Press, 2015), and *Current Controversies in Bioethics* (Routledge, forthcoming). He has given a TED talk in New York and has been featured in many media outlets including *The New York Times* and the BBC. He is the Editor-in-Chief for the *Journal of Moral Philosophy*, a peer-reviewed international journal of moral, political, and legal philosophy.

**William MacAskill** is Associate Professor of Philosophy at Lincoln College, University of Oxford. He's the co-founder of the non-profits Giving What We Can and 80,000 Hours, which have between them raised over $12 million for the most cost-effective charities, with a further $380 million in lifetime-pledged donations.

**Hannah Maslen** is Research Fellow in Ethics at the Oxford Uehiro Centre for Practical Ethics. She works on a wide range of topics in applied philosophy and ethics, from new technologies to moral emotions and criminal justice. Her published work includes a series of articles on brain-intervention technologies, as well as a book on remorse and retribution in criminal sentencing.

**Jeff McMahan** is the White's Professor of Moral Philosophy at Oxford University. His books include *The Ethics of Killing* (Oxford University Press, 2002) and *Killing in War* (Oxford University Press, 2009).

**Ole Martin Moen** is Post-doctoral Fellow in Philosophy at University of Oslo. He works on social issues that have traditionally received relatively little attention from philosophers. His papers have dealt with, among other things, the ethics of prostitution, pedophilia, cryonics, cosmetic surgery, begging, and the suffering of wild animals.

**Seán Ó hÉigeartaigh** is the Executive Director of Cambridge's Centre for the Study of Existential Risk (CSER). He has played a central role in research on long-term AI impacts and risks for the last few years, leading the Oxford Martin Programme on the Impacts of Future Technology from 2011–14, and has recently co-developed the Leverhulme Centre for the Future of Intelligence (Cambridge). His PhD was in genome evolution.

**Russell Powell**, JD PhD, is Assistant Professor of Philosophy at Boston University and Associate Editor of the *Journal of Medical Ethics*. He was formerly an associate of the law firm Skadden, Arps Slate Meagher and Flom LLP.

**Jonathan Pugh** is Post-doctoral Research Fellow in Applied Moral Philosophy on the Wellcome Trust funded project 'Neurointerventions in Crime Prevention: An Ethical Analysis'. He has published research on the ethics of stem-cell research, human enhancement, and autonomy and informed consent in bioethics.

**Theron Pummer** is Lecturer in Philosophy and Director of the Centre for Ethics, Philosophy and Public Affairs, at the University of St Andrews. He was previously Plumer Junior Research Fellow in Philosophy at St Anne's College, University of Oxford. His research interests include well-being and personal identity. Within practical ethics he is especially interested in our obligations to people in extreme poverty and to future generations.

**Janet Radcliffe Richards** is Professor of Practical Philosophy at the University of Oxford, and Distinguished Research Fellow and Consultant at the Uehiro Centre for Practical Ethics. She works widely in practical ethics and is the author of *The Sceptical Feminist* (Routledge, 1980), *Human Nature after Darwin* (Routledge, 2000), and *Careless Thought Costs Lives: the Ethics of Transplants* (Oxford University Press, 2012).

**Regina Rini** is Assistant Professor/Faculty Fellow in the Center for Bioethics at New York University. Before this she held a research fellowship at the Oxford Uehiro Centre for Practical Ethics. She works on the cognitive science of moral judgement, the concept of moral agency, and ethical issues arising from identity-affecting biotechnologies.

**Simon Rippon** is Assistant Professor at Central European University, Budapest, in the Philosophy Department and the School of Public Policy. He has ongoing research interests in practical ethics, reasons, rationality, normativity, and epistemology. His published journal articles include papers on why we should take the means to our ends and on the ethics of procuring organs for transplant.

**Rebecca Roache** was educated at the universities of Leeds and Cambridge, and spent six years as Research Fellow at Oxford University before joining Royal Holloway, University of London, in September 2014. She has diverse philosophical interests that encompass applied ethics, metaphysics, and philosophy of psychiatry. She is currently working on a book about the philosophy of swearing.

**Anders Sandberg** is James Martin Fellow at the Future of Humanity Institute as well as researcher at the Oxford Uehiro Centre for Practical Ethics, the Oxford Centre for Neuroethics, and the Institute of Futures Studies in Stockholm. His main areas of research are enhancement ethics, emerging technology, and global catastrophic risks.

**Julian Savulescu** has held the Uehiro Chair in Practical Ethics at the University of Oxford since 2002. He holds degrees in medicine, neuroscience, and bioethics. He is the Director of the Oxford Uehiro Centre for Practical Ethics as well as the Oxford Centre for Neuroethics. He is also Director of the Institute for Science and Ethics within the Oxford Martin School at the University of Oxford, where he examines the ethical implications of technology affecting the mind, as well as the science of moral decision-making and behaviour.

**Owen Schaefer** is Research Fellow at the National University of Singapore's Centre for Biomedical Ethics. His main academic interests lie in applied ethics. Ongoing research topics include disclosure of incidental findings, responsible data sharing, and the governance of research involving human subjects.

**Joshua Shepherd** is Wellcome Trust Research Fellow (Investigator Award 104347) at the Oxford Uehiro Centre for Practical Ethics, Junior Research Fellow at Jesus College, and James Martin Fellow at the Oxford Martin School. His research concerns issues in the philosophy of mind, cognitive science and action, in moral psychology, and in neuroethics.

**Peter Singer** is the Ira W. DeCamp Professor of Bioethics at Princeton University, and Laureate Professor in the School of Historical and Philosophical Studies at the University of Melbourne. He is perhaps best known for his book *Animal Liberation* (HarperCollins, 1975).

**Walter Sinnott-Armstrong** is Stillman Professor at Duke University in the Philosophy Department, the Kenan Institute for Ethics, and the Center for Cognitive Neuroscience. He publishes widely in ethics, moral psychology and neuroscience, philosophy of law, epistemology, informal logic, and philosophy of religion.

**Lance K. Stell** is Emeritus Professor at Davidson College and Emeritus Professor of Medicine at the University of North Carolina School of Medicine.

**Dominic Wilkinson** is Consultant Neonatologist at the John Radcliffe Hospital, and Associate Professor and Director of Medical Ethics at the University of Oxford Uehiro Centre for Practical Ethics. His is the author or *Death or Disability? The Carmentis Machine and Decision-making for Critically Ill Children* (Oxford University Press, 2013).

**James Williams** is a doctoral candidate at the Oxford Internet Institute and Balliol College, Oxford. His research focuses on the philosophy and ethics of technology design. He has worked in Special Projects at Google and has a background in literature and product design engineering.